T0123593

BIBLE STUDY WORKBOOK

THE PRISON LETTERS
EPHESIANS, PHILIPPIANS, COLOSSIANS, PHILEMON

Paul C. Jones, PhD

WESTBOW
PRESS®
A DIVISION OF THOMAS NELSON
& ZONDERVAN

Copyright © 2018 Paul C. Jones, PhD.

All rights reserved. No part of this book may be used or reproduced by any means, graphic, electronic, or mechanical, including photocopying, recording, taping or by any information storage retrieval system without the written permission of the author except in the case of brief quotations embodied in critical articles and reviews.

WestBow Press books may be ordered through booksellers or by contacting:

WestBow Press
A Division of Thomas Nelson & Zondervan
1663 Liberty Drive
Bloomington, IN 47403
www.westbowpress.com
1 (866) 928-1240

Because of the dynamic nature of the Internet, any web addresses or links contained in this book may have changed since publication and may no longer be valid. The views expressed in this work are solely those of the author and do not necessarily reflect the views of the publisher, and the publisher hereby disclaims any responsibility for them.

Scriptures taken from the Holy Bible, New International Version®, NIV®. Copyright © 1973, 1978, 1984, 2011 by Biblica, Inc.™ Used by permission of Zondervan. All rights reserved worldwide. www.zondervan.com The "NIV" and "New International Version" are trademarks registered in the United States Patent and Trademark Office by Biblica, Inc.™ All rights reserved.

This book is a work of non-fiction. Unless otherwise noted, the author and the publisher make no explicit guarantees as to the accuracy of the information contained in this book and in some cases, names of people and places have been altered to protect their privacy.

Any people depicted in stock imagery provided by Getty Images are models, and such images are being used for illustrative purposes only. Certain stock imagery © Getty Images.

ISBN: 978-1-9736-3292-4 (sc)
ISBN: 978-1-9736-3293-1 (hc)
ISBN: 978-1-9736-3315-0 (e)

Library of Congress Control Number: 2018907910

Print information available on the last page.

WestBow Press rev. date: 07/06/2018

TABLE OF CONTENTS

Ephesians

1

OVERVIEW AND OUTLINE

Who is the Author: _____

When was the book written (B.C., A.D): _____

What number is the book in the New Testament: _____

What number is the book in Canonical Bible: _____

Setting or Location: _____

_____

_____

What Greek goddess had a temple in Ephesus?: _Hint: Diana _____

_____

_____

BOOK BLUEPRINT

- **Unity In Christ:**   Chapters 1 - 3
- **Unity in the Body of Christ:**   Chapters 4 - 6

MAJOR ARGUMENTS

Paul utilizes the term "Ekklesia" or "church" to describe an actual gathering of local Christians on a regular basis, even though this term is also extended to the universal church, the body of believers. Ephesians seems to be concern with the unity of the church, and the ability of the church to live according to the precepts and teachings of Jesus (holiness). Impurity belongs to the past, and being blameless is paramount as one grows and is shaped into the holy temple in the Lord. The church and world seem to come to maturity as each one embraces and encourages love and service. In order for us to live in harmony and in union, we must be in union with Jesus Christ.

Salvation has been extended to humanity through being reconciled to God by Christ Jesus. The death of Christ overcame the divide that existed between Gentiles and Jews, and as a result it created a new humanity that was loving and unified. The process of being restored to God is made through Jesus Christ, providing man, woman and child the opportunity to access God the Father.

The Apostle Paul assures the readers and hearers of what God has brought to fruition while Paul solidifies the identity of believers in Christ. There is no illusion that to follow Christ, means to be removed from the pains and conflicts of the world. Thus, the believers who have been seated with Jesus in the heavenly realms are the same ones who are required to walk in this world and take a stand against opposing powers to uphold the Gospel.

As believers in Jesus Christ, the Holy Spirit (the Spirit of Jesus) guides and enables us to live according to God's will. Therefore, to be able to connect and be directed by the Holy Spirit, Christians have to lay aside self, worldliness, wants and desires, and they must lean completely on the power that comes and is of Jesus Christ. When the response to Jesus is found to be in truth and sincerity, His purpose for humanity becomes the mission, vision, goal and objective that is embraced.

The lordship of Jesus is elevated when God talks about what was consummated when Jesus was raised from the dead. God's plan is revealed through Jesus (vs. 1:10), which brings unity in heaven and earth. Therefore, if a believer is in Christ Jesus, he/she belongs to a system, a movement that extends beyond the boundaries of the universe where everything is in concert, and the concert is in harmony. Hence, all believers become one family in Christ Jesus.

CHURCH UNITY: EPHESIANS 1

CHAPTER BLUEPRINT

GREETING

"Paul, an apostle of Christ Jesus by the will of God[1]. To the saints in Ephesus[2], the faithful in Christ Jesus[3]: Grace and peace to you from God our Father and the Lord Jesus Christ" (vv. 1-2).

---

[1] Time and time again we learn of false teachers and spiritual leaders that had and are leading people astray. Paul is affirming to the church that the ministry and gospel that he is proclaiming if from God. The calling to a role of leadership (i.e., pastor, shepherd, minister, apostle, teacher, or evangelist) should not come from self. It is important that we as believers operate within the blessings and will of God.

[2] The name *Ephesus* is meant to have come from the name *Apasas*, which means "City of the Mother Goddess," which referred to a legend that Ephesus was founded by female warriors. The city was eventually dominated by the Lydians, Persians, Greeks and Romans. The city was the residence for the great Temple of Artemis, the Library of Celsus, and an outdoor theatre (coliseum) for gladiators. This city was also the capital of Asia Minor. Because of its location, the city was the center of trade and commerce. The population of people living in the city was approximately five hundred thousand. Some scholars have argued that during the days of Apostle John, he took the mother of Jesus (Mary) to Ephesus and provided care for her.

[3] The "faithful in Christ Jesus" may provide insight that this letter is not only for the church in Ephesus, but the letter is possibly meant to be circulated among all Christians and surrounding communities.

What is the blessing (v. 1)? _____

_____

What purpose does the blessing serve? _____

_____

Why does the blessing speak of being from the Father and Son (v. 2)? ___

_____

BLESSINGS/REDEMPTION

"Praise be to the God and Father of our Lord Jesus Christ, who has blessed us in the heavenly realms with every spiritual blessings in Christ[4]" (v. 3).

What does this mean to be blessed in the heavenly realms? _____

_____

What are the spiritual blessings? _____

_____

"For He chose us in Him before the creation of the world to be holy and blameless in His sight" (v. 4).

Do we have the choice of being a Christian? _____

_____

When was the decision made? _____
What is God's will toward the chosen? _____

_____

---

[4]   When you have one blessing, you are happy and feel fortunate. However, if you have "every" blessing, you possess all the wonderful benefits (i.e., peace, joy, happiness, patience, prosperity, security, health) that come with having a relationship with Jesus.

📖

"In love, He predestined us to be adopted as His sons through Jesus Christ[5], in accordance with His pleasure and will to the praise of His glorious grace, which He has freely given us in the One he loves" (vv. 5-6).

What was the attitude for which God determine our destiny (v. 5)? _____

What tool do you utilize to determine the destiny of others? _____
_____

Are believers of today considered a lower class because of adoption? ____
_____

Why are we a part of God's family (v. 5)? _____
_____

What is meant by glorious grace (v. 6)? _____
_____

Who is the "One he loves" or "Beloved" (v. 6)? _____
_____

📖

"In Him we have redemption through His blood, the forgiveness of sins, in accordance with the riches of God's grace that He lavished on us with all wisdom and understanding[6]" (vv. 7-8).

Redemption means what (v. 7)? _____
Redemption through blood means what (v. 7)? _____
_____

What are the functions of His blood"?
    1. _____
    2. _____

---

[5] Predestination is not only a common and important theme but it is an act of God upon all mankind and creation. It signifies that God knows (Omniscient) prior to any type of revelation and before time.

[6] Lavish generally refers to being extravagant, excessive, plentiful or generous. However, God through Paul utilizes the word lavish to mean "shower or pour." It's wonderful to know that God loves believers in Christ Jesus in this manner. God demonstrates His love by showering the riches of His grace upon us.

3. _____

4. _____

Is this the same grace spoken of in verse six? _____

_____

God lavished on us with all wisdom and understanding means what (v. 8)? _____

_____

How can we apply this principle of wisdom and understanding in our everyday lives? _____

_____

📖

"And He made known to us the mystery of His will according to His good pleasure[7], which He purposed in Christ, to be put into effect when the times will have reached their fulfillment[8], to bring all things in heaven and on earth together under one head, even Christ" (vv. 9-10).

What is the mystery that God made known (v. 9)? _____

_____

What does it mean to put into effect or dispensation (v. 10)? _____

_____

Who is the head of the family for which all things are under (v. 10)? ____

_____

📖

"In Him we were also chosen, having been predestined according to the plan of Him who works out everything in conformity with the purpose of

---

[7]   The "mystery of His will" refers to God's plan of salvation for mankind through the death and resurrection of Jesus Christ. This plan nullified the separate nations, ethnicity, origins and beliefs of people and brought all persons, Jew and Gentile (all who are not Jewish) together as one people and one body under Christ.

[8]   To be placed in "effect" is closely related to the word translated **dispensation**, which means "house rule." The English word **economy** is derived from this Greek word, which refers to God's arrangement of all history to fulfill His plan.

His will, in order that we, who were the first to hope in Christ, might be for the praise of His glory" (vv. 11-12).

God works things according to the _____ of His will (v. 11).
Who are the first in Christ (v. 12)? _____

_____

How can the first be God's praise (v. 12)? _____

_____

📖

"And you also were included in Christ when you heard the word of truth, the gospel of your salvation. Having believed, you were marked in Him with a seal[9], the promised Holy Spirit, who is a deposit guaranteeing our inheritance until the redemption of those who are God's possession, to the praise of His glory[10]" (vv. 13-14).

How do people today become a part of Christ (v. 13)? _____

_____

How are God's people identified (v. 13)? _____

_____

What does the seal of the Holy Spirit look like? _____

_____

The purpose of the seal is what (v. 14)? _____

PRAYER

"For this reason, ever since I heard about your faith in the Lord Jesus and your love for all the saints, I have not stopped giving thanks for you, remembering you in my prayers" (vv.15-16).

How should your faith be evidenced (v. 15)? _____

_____

_____

[9]   The seal is a mark of possession or ownership that signifies that we are part of God's family, belonging to Christ Jesus.

[10]   A guarantee is an assurance, promise, warranty that secures. Do you have the assurance of inheritance as a child of God?

How should your love be experienced (v. 15)? _____

_____

Pray for those who (v. 16)? _____Hint: Galatians 6:10 _____

_____

When we pray for others we need to do what first (v. 16)? _____

_____

📖

"I keep asking that the God of our Lord Jesus Christ, the glorious Father, may give you the Spirit of wisdom and revelations, so that you may know Him better" (v. 17).

When you pray for others you need to ask God for what? _____

_____

What three elements have been identified in the same sentenced? _____

_____

Jesus and Paul teach us to go to whom in prayer? _____

_____

📖

"I pray also that the eyes of your heart may be enlightened in order that you may know the hope to which He has called you[11], the riches of His glorious inheritance in the saints" (v. 18).

What was the problem with the people's heart? _____

_____

What is the heart? _____

What is the hope? _____

_____

What is the glorious inheritance? _____

---

[11] To have "eyes of the heart" refers to the deep understanding that lies within the inner person or spirit of a person, which possesses divine knowledge and clarification.

"And His incomparably great power for us who believe. That power is like the working of His mighty strength[12], which He extended in Christ when He raised Him from the dead and seated Him at His right hand in the heavenly realms, far above all rule and authority, power and dominion, and every title that can be given, not only in the present age but also in the one to come" (vv. 19-21).

Why is God's power so incomparable (v. 19)? _____

_____

What power of God is Paul talking about (vv. 19-20)? _____

_____

Jesus Christ is seated where (vv. 19-21)? _____

_____

"And God placed all things under His feet and appointed Him to be head over everything for the church, which is His body, the fullness of Him who fills everything in every way" (vv. 22-23).

What does it mean that God placed everything under Jesus' feet (v. 22)? _

_____

Who is the head of the Church (v. 22)? _____

Who is the true body of Christ (v. 22)? _____ Hint: 1 Corinthians 12:12-28 _____

_____

The fullness of Jesus means the what (v. 23)? _____

_____

---

[12] To possess a power that can raise, from death to life, is beyond all human efforts and true imagination. However, as believers and disciples of Jesus, access to the great power of God is available to those who walk by faith in Jesus.

ALIVE IN CHRIST: EPHESIANS 2

CHAPTER BLUEPRINT

GRACE THROUGH FAITH

"As for you, you were dead in your transgressions and sins[13], in which you used to live when you followed the ways of this world and of the ruler of the kingdom of the air, the spirit who is now at work in those who are disobedient" (vv. 1-2).

What does it mean "dead in your transgressions and sins (v. 1)? _____
_____

Who was Paul talking to (v. 1)? _____
What do we mean by "walked" or "live" (v. 2)? _____
_____

What does the ways of the world and the ruler of the kingdom of the air have in common (v. 2)? _____
_____

---

[13]   To be dead in your transgressions and sins means that you have no life. Sin and wrongdoings separate us from the Lord, who is life. Thus, as we participate through words, thought and action in wrongdoings, we become lifeless (dead) and numb to the blessings and grace of God, which is life.

Who is the spirit at work in the disobedient (v. 2)? _____

📖

"All of us also lived among them at one time[14], gratifying the cravings of our sinful nature and following its desires and thoughts. Like the rest, we were by nature objects of wrath" (v. 3).

Name some things that we gratify? _____
_____

How does our mind affect our cravings? _____
_____

What people are the objects of wrath? _____

📖

"But because of his great love for us. God who is rich in mercy[15], made us alive with Christ even when we were dead in transgressions[16]" (vv. 4-5).

What is the difference between love and great love (v. 4)? _____
_____

According to the scriptures we are supposed to be what (v. 4)? _____
You have been saved by what (v. 5)? _____

---

[14] Being a Christian does not mean you are superior to everyone else. There are many people that are kind, generous, and dedicate themselves to helping mankind, but your deeds cannot get you into heaven. All persons have been subject to sin and have lived in sin at one time or another due to the nature (Adam, the instrument of sin) of man. That's why believers must be born again to overcome the world, not into the flesh but into God the Father, through Jesus Christ by the power of the Holy Spirit. We need the gift of faith from God as we surrender to Him and find rest, shelter and peace.

[15] God is the creator of all things, seen and unseen, known and unknown. God has an abundance, an unending supply that is more than we could ever imagine. He possesses a bottomless well of compassion, forgiveness, kindness, sympathy, understanding, generosity and love.

[16] By accepting Jesus Christ as your Lord and Savior, you are no longer bound by the grips of sin and wrongdoings, no longer bound by society and the sinful ways of the world. You now walk by faith in Christ, you walk in the blessings of the Father, and you walk with eyes set on things that are above.

Grace is what in this periscope (v. 5)? _____

📖

"And God raised us up with Christ and seated us with Him in the heavenly realms in Christ Jesus[17], in order that in the coming ages he might show the incomparable riches of His grace, expressed in His kindness to us in Christ Jesus" (vv. 6-7).

How did God raise us up with Christ (v. 6)? _____

To be seated with Christ now means what (v. 6)? _____
_____

When are the "coming ages" (v. 7)? _____
_____

📖

"For it is by grace you have been saved, through faith and this not from yourselves, it is the gift of God[18], not by works, so that no one can boast" (vv. 8-9).

What is the instrument for which we have been saved (v. 8)? _____
Faith is a what (v. 8)? _____
Grace is a what (v. 8)? _____
Can grace be produced from works (v. 9)? _____
If we can boast and take credit, where does that place God (v. 9)? _____
_____

---

[17] God the Father raised Jesus from the dead. Because Christ is now inside of us as believers, God will raise us up to the heavenly realms from the physical constraints of the earthly world and death.

[18] A gift is something that does not have to be repaid. A gift is not something that you earn. A gift is an expression of an appreciated thought, which should yield in return an appropriate response of gratitude, simply by saying the words "thank you" or "I appreciate."

"For we are God's workmanship[19], created in Christ Jesus to do good works, which God prepared in advance for us to do[20]" (v. 10).

We are whose workmanship? _____

Should we try to make a change in people, why or why not? _____

_____

We are all meant to do what? _____

Why or why not is our destiny in our hands? _____

_____

BROUGHT NEAR BY HIS BLOOD

"Therefore, remember that formerly you who are Gentiles by birth and called "uncircumcised" by those who call themselves "the circumcision" (that done in the body by the hands of men), remember that at that time you were separate from Christ, excluded from citizenship in Israel and foreigners to the covenants of the promise[21], without hope and without God in the world" (vv. 11-12).

---

[19]   When we take the time to realize and appreciate that we are not from or of ourselves, but that we are the works of God, it humbles us who have faith in God. It provides an identification that is not governed by the world. It constantly reminds us that we are a needed and precious element in God's full plan. At the same time, it gives us strength, and encourages us to hold our heads up in Christ Jesus as we go about our lives, and as we interact with others and creation itself.

[20]   What is better than the present? It is preordained, predetermined, predestined or in advance. It is so comforting to know that our lives are not something of a whim. God knew us and determined before time the destiny or road that we must travel. Hence, our existence was well thought out, it was planned. It brings solace and joy to our spirit and mind to know that the Lord our God and His work and goal is beyond all measure and conception.

[21]   It is no surprise that as part of human nature and being caught up in the traditions and practices of man, it is easy to think that the blessings of God are for you and those like you only. The Jews thought that the promises of God, the promises of Abraham were solely for the Jews. Praise God, that Jesus brought clarity, understanding and hope. Israel here is not pointing to the nation of Israel, but is referring to the people of God, the family of God which includes all believers in Jesus Christ. Therefore, it is most important that we raise the

What is God constantly calling Christians to do (v. 11)? _____

Why were Gentiles excluded from the covenant and without hope (v. 12)? _____

_____

"But now in Christ Jesus you who once were far away have been brought near through the blood of Christ[22]" (v. 13).
How were Gentiles brought hear? _____

Who are considered today the Gentiles? _____

_____

CHRIST OUR PEACE

"For He himself is our peace, who has made the two one and has destroyed the barrier[23], the dividing wall of hostility. By abolishing in His flesh the law with its commandments and regulations. His purpose was to create in Himself one new mane out of the two thus making peace" (vv. 14-15).

Who is our peace (v. 14)? _____
Who are the two that has been made one (v. 14)? _____

_____

What was the barrier, the dividing wall (v. 14)? _____

_____

spirits of all who have chosen this divine path, regardless if they may be weak or strong in faith.

[22] The blood of Jesus Christ is the instrument or avenue whereby all races, ethnicities and gender can be reunited with the Creator.

[23] Mankind has a natural tendency to place barriers between others who are not of affinity. Thus, creating classifications of superior and inferior, blessed and cursed, good and dross. This is found among the ethnic groups in the world, and also found in the church among those who confess Christ. The barriers of separation and hostility towards one another have been demolished by Jesus, affording peace and unity to be the reigning element.

What kind of walls do you build between you and others? _____
_____

What was the result of Christ's death (v. 15)? _____
_____

📖

"And in this one body to reconcile both of them to God through the cross[24], by which He put to death their hostility. He came and preached peace to you who were far away and peace to those who were near" (vv. 16-17).

What avenue allows the opportunity for us to be reconciled to God (v. 16)? _____
_____

Reconciled means what? _____
_____

God's word is meant for who (v. 17)? _____

📖

"For through Him we both have access to the Father by one Spirit[25]" (v. 18).

God is portrayed how? _____
_____

What is meant by one Spirit? _____

OUR CORNERSTONE

"Consequently, you are no longer foreigners and aliens, but fellow citizens with God's people and members of God's household[26]. Built on the

---

[24] The cross was not just pieces of wood placed together, but the cross was the pavement for which Jesus brought man and God back into relationship.

[25] Again, the Trinity (God the Father, God the Son and God the Holy Spirit) is also revealed and referenced in this verse.

[26] As Believers, we don't have to worry about our citizenship, taking an oath to a flag and country. For those who confess Jesus as Lord and Savior, citizenship now rest in God. We are a people belonging to God and are part of His royal family, who does not require some type of identification tag (SSI number) or

foundation of the apostles and prophets[27], with Christ Jesus himself as the chief cornerstone" (vv. 19-20).

What does it mean to be a citizen (v. 19)? _____

_____

God's household is made up of whom (v. 19)? _____

_____

The foundation of the apostles and prophets is what or whom (v. 20)? ___

_____

What is meant by the chief cornerstone (v. 20)? _____

_____

How the church is today built (v. 20)? _____

_____

"In Him the whole building is joined together and rises to become a holy temple in the Lord[28]. And in Him you too are being built together to become a dwelling in which God lives by His Spirit" (vv. 21-22).

Why do some people claim that their body is the temple of God (v. 21)? _

_____

How does God live within us (v. 22)? _____

_____

---

branding. Do you feel at home when you are participating and recognized in the activities of the world? Or are you at home and at peace knowing that you are a child of the Most High?

[27] This is referring to the church is based upon new spiritualties and variations thereof. But God's house is built upon the word, teachings, legacy and nature of God.

[28] The whole building refers to the body of believers coming together as one solid unit.

MYSTERY TO THE GENTILES: EPHESIANS 3

CHAPTER BLUEPRINT

- Messenger to All (3:1 – 3:13)
- A Prayer (3:14 – 3:21)

MESSENGER TO ALL

"For this reason I[29], Paul, the prisoner of Christ Jesus for the sake of you Gentiles" (v. 1).

How is Paul the prisoner of Christ Jesus? _____

_____

Who is to benefit from Paul's plight? _____

_____

Who is benefiting from your present relationship with Jesus? _____

_____

---

[29]   Paul pauses for a moment to reiterate what and why about his actions and mission.

📖

"Surely you have heard about the administration of God's grace that was given to me for you[30], that is, the mystery made known to me by revelation, as I have already written briefly[31]" (vv.2-3).

What is the implication regarding the Administration of God's grace (v. 2)? _____

_____

Is Paul being sarcastic in his response (v. 2)? _____

What is the administration of God's grace (v. 2)? _____

Why is Paul's message a mystery (v. 3)? _____

_____

How did Paul receive the mystery (v. 3)? _____

Why God's Word is a mystery to today's church member(s)? _____

_____

📖

"In reading this, then, you will be able to understand my insight into the mystery of Christ[32], which was not made known to men in other generations as it has now been revealed by the Spirit to God's holy apostles and prophets[33]" (vv. 4-5).

---

[30] This administration is the stewardship that was given to Paul from God to carry to the Gentiles, to reveal that the promises of God that is made available to the Jews is equally available to the Gentiles, bringing both together as one people of equal status in Jesus and the church.

[31] It is important to keep lines of communication open. The lines of communication may in spoken word, written word or in practice. People absorb or learn through repetition. We do not have the previous writing or letter, but we are aware that there was communication and teaching in the past by Paul. Isn't it wonderful to know that God's grace provides second and third chances for our benefit? Are you giving somebody another chance or have you shut the door?

[32] God works on His own time schedule that does not necessarily agree with mans. God had revealed a considerable amount of knowledge in the past, but ultimate had to wait for a later time, which is the time of Christ Jesus. For there was a special work (the cross) that needed to be completed prior to revelation, Salvation in Jesus Christ is for all, not just Jews, but all who believe.

[33] God gave the mystery of Christ to the ones (Prophets and Apostles) that he ordained and tasked to go out into the world and share the gospel. Today, God

Is Paul talking about a current or past letter (v. 4)? _____

Who or what reveals God's plan (v. 5)? _____

_____

Is salvation available to Israel and Gentiles alike (v. 5)? _____

_____

📖

"This mystery is that through the gospel the Gentiles are heirs together with Israel, members together of one body[34], and sharers together in the promise in Christ Jesus" (v. 6).

What is the shocking news to Israel? _____

_____

📖

"I became a servant of this gospel by the gift of God's grace given me through the working of His power[35]" (v. 7).

Do we have the authority to make ourselves servants of God? _____

_____

---

has given that assignment to all believers. Through your daily walk with God and interaction with society, family, self and resources, the word of God will be passed to all generations and all people.

[34] In Christ Jesus, there is no favorite race or ethnicity over another. God's grace is made available to one race, one family, one body, which is composed of all races, nationalities, gender and age. One of the key words appears to be the word "share," which signifies there is a giving and receiving, a balance, a harmony, a peace in God's will and house.

[35] Paul again reiterates that he is not preaching or acting out of his own power, desires and ambition. Paul makes clear that he is under the authority and power of God. Therefore, the words that are spoken are not his words. Hence, the message can be trusted and valued because the words are the word of the Lord.

📖

"Although I am less than the least of all God's people[36], this grace was given me[37]: to preach to the Gentiles the unsearchable riches of Christ, and to make plain to everyone the administration of this mystery, which for ages past was kept hidden in God, who created all things[38]" (vv. 8-9).

Why is Paul considering himself as the least (v. 8)? _____

_____

Why does God commission many different servants (v. 9)? _____

_____

📖

"His intent was that now, through the church, the manifold wisdom of God should be made known to the rulers and authorities in the heavenly realms[39], according to His eternal purpose which He accomplished in Christ Jesus our Lord" (vv. 10-11).

What is one of the main important purposes of the church (v. 10)? _____

_____

The spreading of the Gospel was decided by whom and when (v. 11)? ___

_____

---

[36] Paul shows his humility by making known his identification that he only operates under the will and power of God's grace (favor), and that he is no better than anyone else, especially considering his past ways of persecution.

[37] You cannot earn God's grace. You cannot purchase God's grace. You are not entitled to God's grace. God's grace, unmerited favor, is a gift of God from God. That's it.

[38] The plan or manner in which God reveals His knowledge, love, wisdom, grace and salvation to man is an element of creation. And God is the author of creation.

[39] God reveals His wisdom in various ways. He purposely chose to reveal through the church, with Jesus being the head and door of the church, the message of eternal salvation that was achieved and finished in Jesus Christ.

"In Him and through faith in Him we may approach God with freedom and confidence[40]. I ask you, therefore, not to be discouraged because of my sufferings for you, which are your glory" (vv. 12-13).

How can you and I approach God (v. 12)? _____

How can your sufferings be the glory for someone else (v. 13)? _____

_____

PRAYER

"For this reason I kneel before the Father[41], from whom His whole family in heaven and on earth derives its name" (vv. 14-15).

Reverence is given in what type or form of communication (v. 14)? _____

_____

Who makes up the whole family (v. 15)? _____

_____

"I pray that out of His glorious riches[42], He may strengthen you with power through His Spirit in your inner being[43], so that Christ may dwell in your

---

[40] The scripture tells us that "Jesus is the way, the truth and the life" (John 14:6). It is only through the blood and resurrection of Jesus that salvation is made possible. The only way to receive this grace, this gift of God is through belief and faith in Jesus. Jesus is the bridge between God and man. Therefore, our access to God is not through aromas, man-made statutes, rituals, sacrifices, people, holidays or traditions. Our access is through Jesus, who is the way.

[41] It is important that in all that we say or do and even think, that we give reverence, honor and glory to God. This includes taking the focus off of self, and showing appreciation and gratitude for who God is, what God has done and what God is doing throughout all creation.

[42] Prayer is not something to be ashamed of. Prayer is communication with God. Prayer should be part of our daily walk with God, not just in the morning, noon and night, but throughout the day as the day changes and brings about new elements.

[43] The inner being is also known as the inner man or spirit (soul is sometimes substituted with spirit). It is the real you without your character or personality.

hearts through faith. And I pray that you, being rooted and established in love, may have power, together with all the saints, to grasp how wide and long and high and deep is the love of Christ[44]" (vv. 16-18).

What is Paul's example of how one should honor God (v. 16)? _____

_____

What comes out of the riches of God (v. 16)? _____

What instrument does God utilize to strengthen (v. 16)? _____

How does Jesus dwell within you (v. 17)? _____

_____

Without faith, it is _____ to please God.

What else should we pray for regarding others (vv. 17-18)? _____

_____

📖

"And to know this love that surpasses knowledge that you may be filled to the measure of all the fullness of God[45]" (v. 19).

What is the purpose from praying in this fashion? _____

_____

What is the fullness of God? _____

_____

It is the true source. Thus, to have strength in your inner being means to have strength in your very essence, which influences the heart (mind) which impacts the body.

[44] The love that is in Christ is immeasurable. You cannot fathom because it is beyond all imagination and knowledge. It has no boundaries, so it cannot be contained or classified. And Christ's love is infinite. It is not limited by the rising of the sun or the going down of the same.

[45] Some interpretations of the "fullness of God" is given to all the gifts that God has instore for man." Another interpretation is that the fullness refers to having Jesus Christ and His Spirit (the Holy Spirit) within you. The most precious gift of God is His son, Jesus. Thus, to have Jesus is to have the utmost of God. God's love for you is so wonderful and pure that He gave us the fullness of Himself in Christ Jesus that we may have life through faith.

"Now to Him who is able to do immeasurably more than all we ask or imagine according to His power that is at work within us[46], to Him be glory in the church and in Christ Jesus throughout all generations, for ever and ever! Amen" (vv. 20-21).

Verses 20 and 21 is also known as a _____ and _____
Verse 20 can be summed in the one word description of God? _____
What power is at work within us (v. 20) _____
Paul shows us that we should end in what type of manner (v. 21)? _____

_____

---

[46] The work of the Lord permeates everything, all people, all places and all time. What God has done, doing and will do deserves all the praise and glory. If that is too much to think about, then just consider and meditate on all the wonderful blessings Jesus has made in your life. In many church services, this scripture is utilized as the Blessing or Benediction that is pronounced at the end of a service.

THE BODY OF CHRIST: EPHESIANS 4

CHAPTER BLUEPRINT
- Maintenance of the Unity   (4:1 – 4:16)
- New Light rather than the Old   (4:17– 4:24)
  a. Not like Gentiles
  b. Christian Tradition
- Practical Injunction, orders   (4:25 – 4:32)

MAINTENANCE OF THE UNITY

"As a prisoner for the Lord, then I urge you to live a life worthy of the calling you have received[47]" (v. 1).

How are we prisoners for the Lord? _____

_____

What does it mean to be a prisoner?
1. _____
2. _____
3. _____

---

[47] As you accept Jesus in your life as your Lord and Savior, God calls you to keep your thoughts, speech and action in a holy manner as prescribed by Him. The past does not matter, but what does matter is the present and the future. Does your every breath lift up the name of Jesus? Are your actions and thoughts pleasing to God? There is no better time than to start right now by going into prayer and asking God for the strength to live according His standards.

4. _____

5. _____

What is the calling that we have received? _____

_____

📖

"Be completely humble and gentle[48]; be patient[49], bearing with one another in love. Make every effort to keep the unity of the Spirit through the bond of peace[50]" (vv. 2-3).

What are 6 ways that we can live this "called" life worthy (vv. 2-3)?

1. _____

2. _____

3. _____

4. _____

5. _____

6. _____

7. _____

Being completely humble means to do what (v. 2)? _____

_____

How do you bear one another in love (v. 2)? _____

_____

---

[48] When we are humble, we think of the needs and benefits of others more than ourselves. Self-ambition and greed go out the door, and we are able to interact with one another with gentleness and kindness, doing to others as we would have them act and treat us.

[49] Longsuffering or patience is a fruit of the spirit, and it is a gift from God. It is not always easy to refrain from acting or responding instantly with and without thought. But if we wait on the Lord, being slow to act, and moving through His power or strength, we will have the staying power to endure and persevere. Patience does not come to us overnight, but it is a work in progress. As we seek for more patience, we must not forget to thank God for what He has already given us.

[50] All persons who truly confess the name of Jesus Christ as Lord are one in the Spirit. As we realize our status, the elements that keep us separated and at each other's throat disappear. And the pledge to love one another as children of God helps keep harmony as the resulting product.

What good is prayer if you are complaining about things? _____

_____

Explain how keeping unity through silence is an excuse for not doing? __

_____

_____

What is the bond of peace (v. 3)? _____

_____

📖

"There is one body and one Spirit, just as you were called to one hope when you were called, one Lord, one faith, one baptism[51], one God and Father of all, who is over all and through all and in all[52]" (vv. 4-6).

Why does Paul start mentioning about one body and one Spirit (v. 4)? __

_____

What is the one hope that we were called (v. 4)? _____

_____

How many Lords, faiths, baptisms and Gods are there (v. 5)? _____

Explain how God is the Father (v. 6):
   I.   Over all?

        _____

   II. Through all?

        _____

   III. In all?

        _____

---

[51]   The act of being baptized is not something that you have to continually repeat at different stages in your life, as according to traditions of man. There is only one true baptism, which is the baptism of the heart and soul in Jesus Christ. Thus, all believers share in this same baptism.

[52]   Isn't it good to know that no matter what takes place, God is in control because He is over all? Whether something may be classified as good or bad, it is still within the workmanship of creation. No matter what the situation, if we look closely and intently, we will see that God is in all that takes place, regardless of the concern, event or location. Take the time to find the reward and blessing, by taking time to discover God in all of your living.

📖

"But to each one of us grace has been given as Christ apportioned it[53]. This is why it says 'When He ascended on high He led captives in His train and gave gifts to men[54]'" (vv. 7-8).

Grace is defined as what? _____

_____

How much grace is given to us (v. 7)? _____

_____

What personal pronoun is being accented to display mean of authority (v. 8)? _____

_____

📖

"What does 'He ascended' mean except that He also descended to the lower earthly regions[55]" (v. 9).

Where is/are the lower earthly regions? _____

_____

How did Jesus ascend and descend? _____

_____

---

[53] It is true that grace can be interpreted as decency or refinement. Hence those are byproducts of true grace. Grace is the unwarranted favor of God which man cannot claim that it comes from self. There are no attached conditions to God's grace. There is no earning or repayment to God's grace, because it is a gift of God through Christ Jesus.

[54] Jesus was not defeated by the grave. Satan and evil did not win. Paul reminds us that Jesus conquered death and rose (ascended) high above, signifying that Satan, demons and all the power of the enemy is under Jesus' feet. Thus, to be on team Jesus, is to be on the winning team. What team are you a member of?

[55] Some have given the interpretation to mean that Jesus descended down into the depths of hell. Others have said that it means that Jesus came down to earth in the form of a man. The main point is that Jesus holds the whole world in the grip of His hands. Hence, there is no place that is outside or blocked from God's vision or touch. No lie or failure to admit can cover up the truth.

"He who descended is the very one who ascended higher than all the heavens, in order to fill the whole universe" (v. 10).

How does Jesus fill the whole universe? _____
_____

"It was He who gave some to be apostles, some to be prophets, some to be evangelists, and some to be pastors and teachers[56], to prepare God's people for works of service[57], so that the body of Christ may be built up" (vv. 11-12).

What are some of the gifts that are not listed (v. 11)? _____
_____

Why did Jesus give us these gifts (v. 12)? _____
_____

In your present service, who are you equipping or preparing? _____
_____

Who builds up the body of Christ (v. 12)? _____
What is the parable about this same principle (Mark 4:26-29)? _____
_____

---

[56] Even though all believers are one in spirit, each person is still the workmanship of the Lord. Each person is still a branch connected to the vine with special gifts, talents, blessings and opportunities that bring honor and glory to the Lord.

[57] This verse gives us the reason for our calling and bestowing of gifts in Christ Jesus. It is not for our benefit, but it is for the benefit of others. To build up or equip is to instruct, encourage, support or be a resource for others, in order that they may have the tools and resources needed to exercise the assignment that has been given to them by God by the power of the Holy Spirit, so that the supremacy and glory of Jesus may be reverenced, along with the church, the body of believers.

📖

"Until we all reach unity in the faith and in the knowledge of the Son of God and become mature, attaining to the whole measure of the fullness of Christ[58]" (v. 13).

What is the ultimate of goal for equipping? _____
_____

This "fullness" has been mentioned how many times between chapter 1 and 4? _____

📖

"Then we will no longer be infants[59], tossed back and forth by the waves, and blown here and there by every wind of teaching and by the cunning and craftiness of men in their deceitful scheming' (v. 14).

When will be no longer infants? _____
What is the problem of infants? _____
_____

How can reading commentaries be helpful and dangerous? _____
_____

---

58 Our call to the ministry does not stop at the time of retirement or when we think we have finished the work. The job continues throughout our lifetime until everyone comes to understand and confess heart, soul and mind that Jesus is the Son of God and salvation is obtained only through Him. Also, the work must continue until all creation comes to the realization that this faith and knowledge is not words of man, but it is the plan and mystery of God for all humanity. For comments regarding "the fullness," please see the note on 3:19.

59 Infants are those who are not mature in the faith of Jesus. Infants in need of an anchor grab ahold of whatever is in reach. Believers that are infants are subject to unknowingly grabbing hold of false teaching and misinterpretations, causing injury, separation, lack of faith, fear and despair, as presented by those who would deceive in order to gain a perspective or advantage that in essence is illusionary and is not real.

"Instead, speaking the truth in love, we will in all things grow up into Him who is the Head, that is, Christ[60]. From Him the whole body, joined and held together by every supporting ligament, grows and builds itself up in love, as each part does its work" (vv. 15-16).

How does the church grow up in Christ (v. 15)? _____

_____

_____

Each person in the Body of Christ is expected to do what (v. 16)? _____

_____

NEW LIGHT RATHER THAN THE OLD

A) NOT LIKE GENTILES

"So I tell you this, and insists on it in the Lord, that you must no longer live as the Gentiles do, in the futility of their thinking[61]" (v. 17).

---

[60] As believers, when we accept Jesus as Lord and Savior, we don't start off as being fully mature in the faith. And, to no surprise, maturity does not happen overnight or in a day or two. It takes time to grow up in Christ. This course is known as sanctification (to be made holy). The process incorporates the many lessons that are to be learned and experienced through life's challenges. It includes time given to studying the word of God, time given to prayer, meditation and listening to God, time given for application of God's word in our lives, time and effort given to be transformed through the remaking of our thought development, and the method of perceiving the visible and the invisible, as we gain strength, direction and revelation by the power of the Holy Spirit.

[61] The Gentiles, who were non-Jews or those who were outside the family of Christ, were exposed, believed and practiced ideologies and theologies that were not in alignment with God. They worshipped false gods that could not benefit them in any manner. There way of thinking was not productive but instead was useless (futile) or vanity. There thinking followed the traditions of man, old laws, and seeing life only through the glasses of their own intellect, science, mythology, tangibility and their humanly senses. What steps are you taking to think and live a life that is holy and pleasing to God? Are you holding on to traditions that the world upholds?

The title of this section suggest what? _____

_____

God is telling us to be what? _____

_____

How should we think? _____

_____

How do we think and live in the new light (Romans 12:1-2)? _____

_____

📖

"They are darkened in their understanding and separated from the life of God because of the ignorance that is in them due to the hardening of their hearts[62]" (v. 18).

What is the problem of the "old" way of thinking? _____

_____

What does it mean to be "darkened"? _____

_____

How we are as Christians sometimes darkened? _____

_____

Hardening of your heart leads to what? _____

_____

📖

"Having lost all sensitivity[63], they have given themselves over to sensuality so as to indulge in every kind of impurity, with a continual lust for more[64]" (v. 19).

---

[62] When a person follows the ways of the world, their ability to think clearly, rationalize, live and interact in holiness is shadowed and blocked. The person lacks the ability to gain knowledge, which leaves him with a mind and heart that can only embrace sin and its characteristics. Thus, the person had no relationship with God and is considered separated.

[63] One of the problems with sin, is that a person loses the ability to be compassionate and understanding. The thoughtfulness of someone else besides themselves has no consideration. In your daily walk, have people referred to you as being cold person? Turn to the Lord that the veil of sin and indifference can be removed that you may be a person of kindness, sympathy and mercy as you abide in Jesus Christ.

[64] Living a life in Christ and walking by faith yields an existence that is fulfilling. When you engage in sin and the products thereof (i.e., money, fame, etc.), you are never satisfied. You can never get enough. The more you receive, the more

Verse 19 can be summed up in the present colloquial saying?

<u>   Walk   </u>   <u>   in   </u>   <u> the </u>   <u>   </u>

Some churches are "cold" because of what? <u>   </u>

<u>   </u>

Sensuality can be found in pleasures of the <u>   </u> and <u>   </u>

B) CHRISTIAN TRADITION

📖

"You, however, did not come to know Christ that way. Surely you heard of Him and were taught in Him in accordance with the truth that is in Jesus[65]" (vv. 20-21).

How did you come to know or learn of Christ (v. 20)? <u>   </u>

<u>   </u>

<u>   </u>

We came to know or learn Jesus in what three ways (v. 21)?

     1. <u>   </u>

     2. <u>   </u>

     3. <u>   </u>

📖

"You were taught, with regard to your former way of life, to put off your old self[66], which is being corrupted by its deceitful desires, to be made new

---

    your eyes hunger and drool for more. Everything that you gain has no staying power, it is temporary and soon passes away. Set your eyes on the unseen. Look to what is permanent and is above. Turn to holiness and discover contentment, peace and unspeakable joy.

[65] Hearing and learning of God comes through the word of God by those who proclaim the Truth as sent and directed by God. By the assignment of Jesus to Christians and powered by the Holy Spirit, believers are to go out into the world and share the gospel through speech and actions to all that they interact with. The results are displayed in loyal obedience to God, people finding salvation, building up of the church and righteous living.

[66] Getting rid of the "old self" is like freeing yourself from worn clothing, and the dirty and nasty things of the world. What you thought, how you acted in

in the attitude of your minds, and to put on the new self, created to be like God in true righteousness and holiness" (vv. 22-24).

What were you taught (vv. 22-23)?

1. _____

2. _____

3. _____

What is the "truth that is in Jesus (v. 24)? _____

PRACTICAL INJUNCTION (ORDERS)

"Therefore each of you must put off falsehood and speak truthfully to his neighbor[67], for we are all members of one body" (v. 25).

What must each of us do to our neighbors? _____

Who are our neighbors? _____

---

the past, the places you use to frequent, types of entertainment, the friends you use to associate with, the means of criticizing and passing judgment, ignorance, misinterpretation and perceptions, and walking without hope are all part of the "old self." When a person accepts Jesus Christ as Lord and Savior, the old things become obsolete and a new way of living, by the standards and means of God, takes over. The days become brighter with nourishment and aspirations for the future, and joy and satisfaction now becomes a reality and a reflection of self.

[67] What is there to gain from lying to one another? Lying results, in distrust, hurt and pain. Lying yields destruction, disappointments, despair, division, and death. In many cases, one who engages in lies cannot remember one lie to another. So, to cover up, the person continues to lie and ultimately creates a bed of nails to rest upon. In the church, we are all members of one body which is Christ Jesus. So no rationalization or logic can give purpose for falsehood. There is no reason or need to lie or pretend.

"In your anger do not sin[68]. Do not let the sun go down while you are still angry, and do not give the devil a foothold" (vv. 26-27).

Is it okay to be angry at times (v. 26)? _____

While angry, we should not what (v. 26)? _____

How does the devil gain control in our lives (vv. 26-27)? _____

_____

"He who has been stealing must steal no longer, but must work, doing something useful with his own hands, that he may have something to share with those in need[69]" (v. 28).

Why do we need to change our ways? _____

What is the objective in the following verses (vv. 12-13, 28)? _____

_____

---

[68] Anger is a response of an emotion or feeling. Anger itself is not necessarily a bad thing. Anger can bring about self-reflection, a review of the situation, forgiveness, repentance and the need for holy intervention. God through Paul is emphasizing that when anger arises, we need to make sure that it does not get out of hand or overcomes us, whereby we open the door, knowingly or unknowingly, to the enemy. When anger surfaces, turn to the Lord and ask Him for help to change your heart.

[69] There is nothing wrong with helping persons who are in need. Our attitude should be one of hospitality and generosity. When we work for our benefits and look beyond ourselves and to the benefits of others, the selfish acts of stealing and misappropriation fade away, and the joy of giving fills the soul. Did you experience meaning and purpose when you were able to help someone from your own resources who was in need?

📖

"Do not let any unwholesome talk come out of your mouth, but only what is helpful for building others up according to their needs, that it may benefit those who listen" (v. 29).

How do we control our mouths? _____

_____

Your words should benefit those who (v. 29)? _____
Silence can be heard by whom and benefits whom? _____

📖

"And do not grieve the Holy Spirit of God, with who you were sealed for the day of redemption" (v. 30).

To "grieve" the Holy Spirit means to what? _____

_____

We were given the Holy Spirit for what reason? _____

_____

📖

"Get rid of all bitterness, rage and anger, brawling and slander, along with every form of malice" (v. 31).

We are to get rid or what?

1. _____ , which is, _____
2. _____ , which is, _____
3. _____ , which is, _____
4. _____ , which is, _____
5. _____ , which is, _____
6. _____ , which is, _____

📖

"Be kind and compassionate to one another, forgiving each other, just as Christ God forgave you[70]" (v. 32).

We are to what?

1. _____
2. _____
3. _____

What is the message for the church and the equipping/preparing the saints? _____
_____

---

[70]   It is not enough just to say "I'm sorry" or "I apologize." When we forgive, we should no longer count the incidence against. Our response should be one of mercy with understanding, in order to restore the injured party to state of normality. This exercise is not to be performed only once, but it is an action that needs to be practice on a continual basis, just as you have been continually forgiven by God.

IMITATORS: EPHESIANS 5

CHAPTER BLUEPRINT:

- Moving In Love   (5:1 – 5:7)
- Living In Light   (5:8– 5:14)
- Walking In Wisdom   (5:15 – 5:21)
- Husbands and Wives   (5:22 – 5:33)

MOVING IN LOVE

"Be imitators of God[71], therefore, as dearly loved children" (v. 1).

Who are we supposed to imitate? _____

How does sanctification fit into this imitation picture? _____

_____

How are we supposed to imitate? _____

_____

---

[71] Because God is everything, it can be scary when we think about how a person can imitate Him who is so great. God is not trying to tell us to be creators as He was, but God is saying through Paul that we need to see life and live life through the eyes and means of self-sacrificial love. Our love for man and creation should go beyond self, should extend beyond affection and acceptance, and should go further than mere giving. Our love should work to benefit others regardless of another person's status or plight. The bible tells us to be like Christ in our thinking and our actions. Christ is love. God is love. Let's change our ways and embrace the meaning, purpose, exercise and product, imitating and loving others as God has and does. Let us be imitators of Jesus Christ.

"And live a life of love, just as Christ loved us and gave Himself up for us as a fragrant offering and sacrifice to God" (v. 2).

How are we supposed to walk or live? _____

_____

How did Christ love us? Hint: 1 Corinthians 13:4-7
1. _____
2. _____
3. _____
4. _____
5. _____
6. _____
7. _____
8. _____
9. _____
10. _____
11. _____
12. _____
13. _____

What did Christ do for us? _____

_____

How was the offering fragrant or sweet smelling? _____

_____

"But among you there must not be even a hint of sexual immorality[72], or of any kind of impurity[73], or of greed, because these are improper for God's holy people' (v. 3).

---

[72] Sexual immorality consists of impurity, lust, prostitution, orgies, fornication, homosexuality, rape and assault.

[73] Impurity is not solely subject to the physical anatomy, but includes the heart, soul, thoughts, speech, desires and admirations. If impurity and sexual immorality is active in your life, then you need to acknowledge it, turn from your ways, and

What type of sexual immorality was Paul referring to? _____

_____

How is this type of sexual immorality viewed as moral by the world? ___

_____

📖

"Nor should there be obscenity, foolish talk or coarse joking[74], which are out of place, but rather thanksgiving. For of this you can be sure: No immoral, impure or greedy person, such a man is an idolater, has any inheritance in the kingdom of Christ and of God" (vv. 4-5).

What is meant by foolish talk (v. 4)? _____

_____

Foolish talk or coarse talking is the product of what? _____
What is fitting of God's people (v. 4)? _____
What will the idolater inherit (v. 5)? _____

Are there any biblical examples of Idolaters inheritance?
1. _____
2. _____
3. _____
4. _____

_____

seek the healing grace of God. The good news or blessing is that God said He would heal His people (II Chronicles 7:14).

[74] Sometimes we joke around, intentionally and unintentionally, and speak the words of the society in a manner that is not becoming of a believer and servant of Christ, unaware of the possible negative consequences. The opportunity of danger is two-fold. First, the inner person (spirit) of the believer is unconsciously injured. Second, the world appropriates the wrong interpretation and impression of a Christian. Hence, the Christian life, with its values and sensitivity are compromised along with the message of the gospel of Jesus Christ. When finding oneself in this type of situation, it is good to be slow to speak and to find elements of gratitude in the situation that can bring about honor, glory and praise to God.

"Let no one deceive you with empty words[75], for because of such things God's wrath comes on those who are disobedient. Therefore do not be partners with them" (vv. 6-7).

What is one of the major task of the world (v. 6)? _____

How do people deceive another (v. 6)? _____

_____

What was the deception in the Church of Ephesus? _____

_____

How are people deceived in the church? _____

_____

The result of not obeying God is what (v. 7)? _____

LIVING IN LIGHT

"For you were once darkness, but now you are light in the Lord. Live as children of light (for the fruit of the light consists in all goodness, righteousness and truth) and find out what pleases the Lord" (vv. 8-10).

Who were once darkness (v. 8)? _____

How have we become light in the Lord (v. 8)? _____

_____

How do Children of Light live (v. 8)? _____

_____

What are the Fruits of the Spirit?

    1. _____

    2. _____

    3. _____

---

75   God through Paul continues His counseling by advising that you should not be buddies or companions with those whose speech are not spiritually edifying or uplifting, and our filed with deceit and lies. Be clear to understand that this caveat is not saying that you cannot interact with those who are outside the family of God, but as a person living in the light and blessings of the Lord, you should be careful not to be in support of words and actions of the disobedient or non-believers.

4. _____

5. _____

6. _____

7. _____

8. _____

9. _____

The Fruits of the Spirit are found in what three elements (v. 9)?

1. _____

2. _____

3. _____

What is the second command of God (v. 10)? _____

_____

What pleases the Lord? Hint: Romans 12:1-2

_____

📖

"Have nothing to do with the fruitless deeds of darkness, but rather expose them[76]. For it is shameful even to mention what the disobedient do in secret" (vv. 11-12).

What should we do with fruitless or unfruitful work (v. 11)? _____

_____

What should we do with deeds of darkness (v. 11)? _____

_____

---

[76] In this verse, sin is called "deeds of darkness." Sin doesn't produce fruit, much less good fruit. Sin, including telling lies, stands in conflict and opposition to God. Therefore, as believers, we should not waste any time or energy with deeds or elements of the dark. We should avoid them at all cost. As a Christian, you no longer carry yourself and participate in the things that you use to. You now walk, talk, think and live in the light, Jesus Christ. Remember, sin thrives in deceit. It works in areas that undisclosed, in the shadows or in secret. Sin has a way of changing its face so that you don't recognize it on the surface in order for sin to get a grip on you. Thus, when confronted with sin, you must call sin for what it is and call on the Lord. And that, my friend, is exposing.

What is the problem of being silent about the darkness? _____
_____

Why is it shameful to casually talk about disobedience (v. 12)? _____
_____

What is the fruit of gossip? _____
_____

📖

"But everything exposed by the light becomes visible, for it is light that makes everything visible. This is why it is said 'Wake up, O sleeper, rise from the dead, and Christ will shine on you'" (vv. 13-14).

What is the light (v. 13)?

1. _____
2. _____
3. _____
4. _____

Visible or manifest is referring to what (v. 14)? _____
Part "b" of this 14th verse is previously stated where in Isaiah? _____

WALKING IN WISDOM

"Be very careful, then how you live, not as unwise but as wise[77], making the most of every opportunity, because the days are evil" (vv. 15-16).

---

[77] Keeping your eyes open, being aware and informed of your surroundings and environment is sensible and wise. Sin is ever present today in society, media politics, schools, church, and home. We must not sit back, relax and take our time in this endeavor, but we need to get on top of it immediately. Don't jump at everything that pops up without giving some thought and weighing it out. Stand it up against the word of God and act or respond according to God's word and His teachings. Every opportunity in the past, present and future possesses two roads that you can take. Each road leads in a different direction with opposing results or consequences to the other road. The choice to embrace sin, to live foolishly and reckless or the choice to live holy according to God's ordinance or manner is in your hands.

How should we live (v. 15)? _____

How do you live wisely (v. 16)? _____

_____

_____

"Therefore do not be foolish, but understand what the Lord's will is[78]. Do not get drunk on wine, which leads to debauchery[79]. Instead, be filled with the Spirit" (vv. 17-18).

What does it mean when it says "foolish" or "unwise" (v. 17)? _____

_____

How do we receive understanding of God's will? _____

_____

Why was becoming drunk a problem for the Ephesians (v. 18)? _____

_____

We should be always filled with what (v. 18)? _____

"Speak to one another with psalms, hymns and spiritual songs[80]. Sing and make music in your heart to the Lord, always giving thanks to God the Father for everything, in the name of our Lord Jesus Christ" (vv. 19-20).

---

[78] God's will is made known to man through His word. It is paramount as believers, that we spend time studying His word, meditating on His word and praying on His word in order that we may gain understanding of His word. Complete understanding does not come over night, but it is a work in progress that yields blessings after blessings.

[79] Debauchery is another way of saying wickedness. When a person consumes too much alcohol, their thinking and perception becomes impaired, whereby they no longer possess the strength and knowhow to make the appropriate decision or act in the most suitable manner. It is better to be filled with the Holy Spirit, God's Spirit which keeps you align, proper and in a state of increasing spiritual strength.

[80] Do you always complain or talk negative when you communicate with others? The Lord tells us that our speech, our interactions with one another should be with a positive tone, loving heart, and melodies and words that uplift and edify. Our communication with the Lord should be seasoned with praise, adoration, reverence and thanksgiving that shows our appreciation for who He is, what He

What is the result of being filled with the Spirit (v. 19)? _____

_____

What things should we give thanks for (v. 20)? _____
How should we show or express our appreciation or gratitude (v. 20)? ___

_____

_____

📖

"Submit to one another out of reverence for Christ[81]" (v. 21).

Who should we submit to (v. 21)? _____
Why should we submit to one another (v. 21)? _____

_____

HUSBANDS AND WIVES

"Wives, submit to your husbands as to the Lord[82]. For the husband is the head of the wife as Christ is the head of the church, His body, of which He is the Savior. Now as the church submits to Christ, so also wives should submit to their husbands in everything" (vv. 22-24).

How should wives submit to their husbands (v. 22)? _____

_____

---

has done, what He is doing and what He will do in the future. It has been stated that when praises go up, blessings come down.

[81] The world loves to step on you by telling you to submit to the higher authority because they are your boss, or they are the one who is in charge, or they are the head of the house, or it is there show. But scripture tells us to submit for another reason. Scripture tells believers to submit out of respect and devotion to Christ, just as Jesus the Son submitted to God the Father.

[82] Members of the church love to check out the theology and philosophy of a pastor or leader by discovering the viewpoint or interpretation of this verse. Women have been victims over the years because of submission. They have suffered abuse, bullying and injury at the hands of misinterpretation of other men and women. This verse is not telling wives that your husband has the right to do whatever he wants with you and that you have no voice in the matter or situation. But this verse is saying that submission should be in alignment with the word of God and it should be a reflection of respect to the Lord.

The husband being the head of the wife also reflects what about women (v. 23)? _____

_____

Husband and wife are compared to what (v. 23)? _____

_____

How does the church submit to Christ (v. 24)? _____

_____

📖

"Husbands, love your wives[83], just as Christ love the church and gave Himself up for her to make her holy, cleansing her by the washing with water through the word, and to present her to Himself as a radiant church, without stain or wrinkle or any other blemish, but holy and blameless. In this same way, husbands ought to love their wives as their own bodies. He who loves his wife loves himself. After all, no one ever hated his own body, but he feeds and cares for it, just as Christ does the church" (vv. 25-29).

How are husbands supposed to love their wives (vv. 25-28)?
    1. _____
    2. _____
    3. _____
    4. _____
    5. _____

How are Christians supposed to present the local church?
    1. _____
    2. _____
    3. _____

---

[83] The love for a wife should not be in pretense. The love for a wife should not be embodied in the physical, but should embrace the entire person (physical psychological and spiritual). The love should reach and give reverence to the depths of the wife's essence who was created by God with the blessings of God. This type of love is self-sacrificing, holds no wrong and is edifying. The love and reverence should yield prayer and thanksgiving to the Lord. In what manner do you love your wife? Do you value her body as much as you value yours? How do you show your love and respect for God's church?

4. _____

5. _____

6. _____

He who loves his wife loves himself means what (v. 28)? _____

_____

How do you care for the body of your spouse (v. 29)? _____

_____

📖

"For we are members of His body[84]" (v. 30).

As believers, we are members of what? _____

📖

"For this reason a man will leave his father and mother and be united to his wife, and the two will become one flesh[85]" (v. 31).

Through marriage, a husband and a wife become what (v. 31)? _____

_____

As a member of God's church we become one with who (v. 31)? _____

_____

---

[84] Does the membership to Christ's body only allow certain genders, ethnicities, ages or family status? As believers in Jesus, we all have become part of Christ's body bringing together our various gifts and talents bestowed to us.

[85] What is good for one is also good for the other. What is bad for one is also bad for the other. Through marriage, the husband and wife come together as one unit. Thus, the effects (whims and blessings, good and bad) of life impacts the husband just as much as the wife, and vice versa. When we become members of God's church our actions effect the church, and the church effects our actions. The two have become one.

"However, each one of you also must love his wife as he loves himself, and the wife must respect her husband[86]" (v. 33).

The wife must do what and how (v. 33)? _____

_____

_____

---

[86] It doesn't matter which way you turn it or flip it, whether it could be upside down, sideways or even crooked. It is not dictated or limited by status, time or place. The common denominator or ingredient in love, and is a product and result of love, seems to be built around this one word, topic and action. And that is respect or reverence.

SPIRITUALITY: EPHESIANS 6

CHAPTER BLUEPRINT

- Children and Parents   (6:1 – 6:4)
- Slaves and Masters   (6:5 – 6:9)
- Armor of God   (6:10 – 6:20)
- Greetings   (6:21 – 6:24)

CHILDREN AND PARENTS

"Children, obey your parents in the Lord, for this is right. Honor your father and mother, which is the first commandment with a promise[87]" (vv. 1-2).

Place the right column in the left, according to the order of Submission/ Covenant and or Priority

1. _____   Jesus
2. _____   Man or Woman

---

[87]   This verse shows that there is a give and take relationship between parents and children, and that neither are independent of each other. The interaction between the two should be in a manner that benefits all. When a child follows the instruction and teaching of the parent, elder or the one in charge, whether or not the child agrees with the directive, the child is obeying. When through the obedience of a child, appreciation and gratitude are discovered by the child and extended to the parents, the child is giving honor by displaying respect and reverence.

3. _____	God
4. _____	Marriage
5. _____	Children
6. _____	Family
7. _____	Job / Career
8. _____	Social Activities

Children are to obey who (v. 1)? _____

The attitude of the child should be obedience as in obeying who (v. 1)? _

This is right means what (v. 1)? _____
_____

Children are to honor their _____ and _____

Does honor mean the same thing as obey (vv. 1-2)? _____
_____

How can this be the first commandment (v. 2)? _____
_____

📖

"That it may go well with you and that you may enjoy long life on the earth[88]" (v. 3).

What is the promise? _____
_____

---

[88] God made a promise (Deut. 5:16), that if a child respects (honors) their parents through thought, words and action, God would bless the child by making their life (days) on earth long. Also, the blessings of God would follow them throughout their life. Thus, the household, parent and child, would become recipients of God's wonderful blessings. This command is so simple. It doesn't require a lot of energy, thought or sacrifice. The command calls one to do what is right in the eyes of the Lord. And it falls in line with the greatest commandment of God. It directs us to treat each other with respect, and in the manner for which we want to be treated (Matt. 22:38-39).

📖

"Fathers, do not exasperate your children, instead, bring the up in the training and instruction of the Lord[89]" (v. 4).

What does it mean to exasperate or provoke? _____

_____

What authority did the child have in the home in Paul's day? _____

_____

The purpose of training child is to help them? _____

What are some means to help a child grow in the Lord?

1. _____
2. _____
3. _____
4. _____
5. _____
6. _____

What are some ways to help children grow inside the church?

1. _____
2. _____
3. _____
4. _____
5. _____
6. _____

---

[89] Parents possess wisdom and history of experience to be shared. Once in a while, frustration of unmet or unfulfilled expectations surfaces and is directed toward the children. God calls parents to make sure that negative emotions and disappointments do not get in the way of responsibility. The words, teachings and instructions that ae shared with children should be that which will build up the identity, character, confidence and spirit of a child as they continue to mature in Christ and in body.

Slaves and Masters

"Slaves, obey your earthly masters with respect and fear, and with sincerity of heart, just as you would obey Christ[90]. Obey them not only to win their favor when their eye is on you, but like slaves of Christ, doing the will of God from your heart" (vv. 5-6).

What are other names for slaves (v. 5)?
1. _____
2. _____

Why is there an emphasis on the type of master (v. 5)? _____
Are the following words Respect (reverence), Fear (trembling), and Sincerity (genuineness) meant to be interpreted separately or as a unit? _____
With what attitude are slaves required to be obedient (v. 5)? _____
_____

In practice, when do slaves usually obey their masters (v. 6)? _____
_____

In practice, when do Christians usually obey God? _____
_____

Slaves are to obey with the locus of what (v. 6)? _____
_____

"Serve wholeheartedly, as if you were serving the Lord, not men[91], because you know that the Lord will reward everyone for whatever good he does, whether he is slave or free" (vv. 7-8).

---

[90] This verse is not supporting slavery or is it denying the existence of slavery. Slavery didn't begin when people were brought over the Atlantic Ocean to America, as taught in some cultures and circles of society. Slavery existed well before. Slave is synonymous with the word Servant. God ask that if you are in a position of service or slavery, perform the service to the best of your ability (heart), whether in agreement or not. Act in a manner that brings reverence, respect and thanksgiving, because through your efforts, you are fulfilling God's plan whereby God will receive the glory.

[91] The attitude for which we work or serve is very important. If we serve with the attitude that we trying to please man, disappointment, anger and failure may

Serving wholeheartedly means to serve how (v. 7)? _____

Who is the one that will reward you (v. 8)? _____
Should mankind skip rewarding others because of the acts of God? _____

📖

"And masters, treat your slaves in the same way. Do not threaten them, since you know that He who is both their Master and yours is in heaven[92], and there is no favoritism with Him" (v. 9).

There should be mutual _____
between Masters and Slaves.
How do slaves show favoritism to masters, and vice versa? _____

ARMOR OF GOD

"Finally, be strong in the Lord and in His mighty power. Put on the full armor of God so that you can take your stand against the devil's schemes[93]" (vv. 10-11).
What is God's mighty power (v. 10)? _____
How many ways can we be strong in God's power? _____
Why do we need protection or full protection (v. 11)? _____

---

be a byproduct. But if we serve with the mindset that we are serving the Lord, we perform at a higher level, giving our best where success is a reality and the Lord, not man, is glorified and God rewards with benefits that are not subject to decay or rot.

[92] Remember to treat everyone fairly because we all have someone higher than us, and that is God, that we have to answer to for what is done here on earth.

[93] Sometimes we wonder why we seemed to be attacked by the enemy and the enemy gains some ground. Prayer is very good, but it is just partial armor. God tells us to put on the "full" or "whole" armor, so we can hold grounded, anchored, and not be moved by whatever the Devil or the enemy throws at us. That means, it takes more than just prayer. Believers need to be covered entirely with every piece of the armor to shield off any advances.

"For our struggle is not against flesh and blood[94], but against the rulers, against the authorities, against the powers of this dark world and against the spiritual forces of evil in the heavenly realms" (vv. 12-13).

Who is the enemy that we fight against (v. 12)?

1. _____

2. _____

3. _____

4. _____

The song writer stated "after you've done all you can, you just (v. 13)? ___

"Stand firm then, with the belt of truth buckled around your waist[95], with the breastplate of righteousness in place[96]" (v. 14).

How do we gird ourselves with the "belt of Truth"? _____

_____

How do we wear the breastplate of righteousness? _____

_____

---

[94] The battles that believers are confronted with are not of man although realized and orchestrated through man. Man is directed by higher powers and used as an instrument to carry the attacks out. Believers are told to love one another. However, we should not embrace or condone the sin that exist and is displayed. Remember, man is a spiritual being, and forces or powers that are at work are spiritual (Satan, fallen angels, sin).

[95] One of the means of strength in a Christian comes from being truthful. A believer can't fight off lies if untruths are proceeding out of the mouth. The tunic worn back then, was loose and had loose ends. It had to be tied around the waist in order to protect. God is saying through Paul that we need to protect ourselves by securing our speech with truth.

[96] The breastplate was a piece of heavy material or leather that covered the vital organs. Our heart and soul are spiritually vital. The manner in which we live and interact with society and creation impacts the heart and soul. Christians are called to live a life, seen and unseen, that is good in the eyes of the Lord.

📖

"And with your feet fitted with the readiness that comes from the gospel of peace[97]" (v. 15).

How do you fit your feet with the gospel of peace? _____
_____

📖

"In addition to all this, take up the shield of faith[98], with which you can extinguish all the flaming arrows of the evil one" (v. 16).

How do you take up the shield of faith? _____
(hint: Proverbs 3:5) _____

What is the purpose of the shield? _____
_____

📖

"Take the helmet of salvation and the sword of the Spirit, which is the word of God[99]" (v. 17).
The helmet is our _____ of our salvation no matter what doubt or discouragement comes.

---

[97]   Soldiers use to wear boots with nails in them to grip the ground. The Christian walk should be grounded in the word of God and not by traditions, rituals, and sacraments of man. This steady and firm walk can only be obtained through regular studying and meditation of God's word, which results in being like a rooted tree in the midst of a flowing waters (Psalms 1:3).

[98]   The word of God tells believers that it is impossible to please God or stand without faith or belief. It is a must for constant belief and trust in knowing that God is God, God is in control, and all supreme power belongs to and is in God's hands. Surrendering yourself, and the situation to God because of faith, and depending on God's grace is crucial. Therefore, are shield of belief or faith must be placed before us protecting our entire being.

[99]   Our spirit directly effects our mind and thinking, which is the central control center of our body. If our spirit is not right, than our minds will not be right, and our actions will harmonize, as well. In order for our spirit to be right, we must possess the weapon that permeates all matter, and that is the sword. The metal sword was the soldier's weapon, and the word of God is our spiritual weapon.

What is the weapon that we Christians use to fight with? _____

_____

📖

"And pray in the Spirit on all occasions with all kinds of prayers and requests[100]. With this in mind, be alert and always keep on praying for all the saints" (v. 18).

How do we pray in the Spirit? _____

_____

What is the final piece of armor and/or advice? _____

📖

"Pray also for me, that whenever I open my mouth[101], words may be given me so that I will fearlessly make known the mystery of the gospel, for which I am an ambassador in chains. Pray that I may declare it fearlessly, as I should" (vv. 19-20).

Why should you pray for other Believers (vv. 19-20)? _____

_____

An Ambassador is what (v. 20)? _____

_____

---

[100] Believers are called to prayer in different ways (i.e. gratitude, petition, praise, etc.). In one of the prison letters of Paul, God tells us through Paul (Phil. 4:6) that we should not be eager about anything and that we should go to God in prayer regarding our situation or concern. Discernment, strength and blessings come through prayer by the power of the Holy Spirit. It is paramount to keep the whole armor of God intact and covering self, that prayer must become a constant activity everyday knowing that prayer is the instrument to connect with God.

[101] Sometimes earthly situations may cause a hindrance or a state of hesitation on the behalf of believers sharing the word of God. As Christians, we should pray for the strength of believers who will testify and share the gospel that they may have the power of the Holy Spirit to overcome the uncertainty or any obstacle that stands in their path.

GREETINGS/BLESSINGS

"Tychicus, the dear brother and faithful servant in the Lord, will tell you everything, so that you also may know how I am and what I am doing. I am sending him to you for this very purpose, that you may know how we are, and that he may encourage you" (vv. 21-22).

What is inferred about Christian action (v. 21)? _____

_____

Why was Paul sending Tychicus out (v. 22)? _____

_____

When we see a fellow believer under attack, what are we called to do? ___

_____

📖

"Peace to the brothers, and love with faith from God the Father and the Lord Jesus Christ. Grace to all who love our Lord Jesus Christ with an undying love" (vv. 23-24).

How does Paul reemphasize the Lordship of Jesus (v. 23)? _____

_____

Who is the blessing directed to (v. 24)? _____

Philippians

1
OVERVIEW AND OUTLINE

Who is the Author: _____

When was the book written (B.C., A.D): _____

From what location was the book written? _____

What number is the book in the New Testament: _____

What number is the book in Canonical Bible: _____

Setting or Location: _____

_____

Philippi was taken from what ancient colony in Macedonia? _____

The name Philippi means what? _____

Where did the name Philippi come from? _____

Who was the father of Alexander the Great? _____

Even though the city had the same rights as the cities of Italy, including Roman law, Roman citizenship and exemption from taxes, what was the official language of this colony? _____

Because of the endings at (3:1) and (4:8), many scholars and theologians argue that this book is a compilation of? _____ books or writings.

BOOK BLUEPRINT

- **Suffering & Serving:**   Chapters 1 - 2
- **Legalism and Giving:**   Chapters 3 - 4

> NOTE: Wherever people gather together, no matter what the period of time may be, it seems that the people gather or organize themselves into groups. The groups construct obstructions and operate within the given barriers according to the principles established from within. As a result, segregation becomes prevalent on the basis of ethnic, social, religious and racial lines.

MAJOR ARGUMENTS

One of the great pleasures as a believer in Jesus Christ is that you can have the weighty gifts of contentment, peace, and composure no matter what situation you find yourself in. This joy originates out of the personal relationship one has with Christ Jesus and the reliance in the strength of the Holy Spirit, and is manifest in our daily service to creation.

As Christians grow in the Lord, it becomes evident that humanity is not as independent as the world projects even though independence is a character that the world demands. Therefore, it appears that it is easy for a believer to try to do things on their own. However, God encourages us that we need each other, and that we need to work with one another. God elicits partnerships in the gospel.

When we are alone or in the presence of someone else, it is not enough for a person to state their belief. In fact, one could say that it is not enough for individuals to come together periodically and worship. However, as Christians mature in spirit and in truth, it becomes paramount that Christians seek the knowledge of Jesus Christ, as well as understanding, that as believers in Christ and heirs of God, we might have the wisdom and the discernment to live a life that is holy and pleasing to God.

JOY IN AFFLICTION: PHILIPPIANS 1

CHAPTER BLUEPRINT

- Greeting   (1:1 – 1:2)
- Thanksgiving and Prayer   (1:3 – 1:11)
- Proclamation   (1:12 – 1:18)
- Real Living   (1:19 – 1:26)
- Suffering   (1:27 – 1:30)

GREETING

"Paul and Timothy[102], servants of Christ Jesus. To all the saints in Christ Jesus at Philippi[103], together with the overseers and deacons: Grace and peace to you from God our Father and the Lord Jesus Christ" (vv. 1-2).

Why does Paul identify himself and Timothy as servants (v. 1)? _____

_____

Who was the book/letter written to (v. 1)? _____

_____

---

[102] Timothy was a close associate of Paul that studied and was guided by Paul. Timothy was thought of as his brother, a peer in the servanthood of Jesus. Ministering to people by the power of the Holy Spirit can through words and/ or actions. You don't always have to be in the direct presence of someone else to help them. Prayer is an awesome tool.

[103] Philippi was a place originally known as Trace, but later renamed after Phillip II. It had diverse cultures and social levels. The Jew population was low with no synagogue in the city. Philippi was located in the Roman province of Macedonia on the Egnatian Way, which is an extension of the Apian Way (a major road).

Overseers and Deacons can be equated with whom of today (v. 1)? _____
Hint: (1 Tim. 3:1-7 & Titus 1:5-9) _____

_____

The greeting is also a what (v. 2)? _____

THANKSGIVING AND PRAYER

"I thank my God every time I remember you" (v. 3).

What should we do first and foremost? _____
When we reflect on others, what should our attitude be? _____

_____

📖

"In all my prayers for all of you, I always pray with joy[104]" (v. 4).

When we pray for others, our attitude should be what? _____
How can be joyful about someone when they are doing wrong to you? __

_____

How can we partner with the messengers of God? _____

_____

📖

"because of your partnership in the gospel from the first day until now, being confident of this, that He who began a good work in you will carry it on to completion until the day of Christ Jesus[105]" (vv. 5-6).

---

[104] Joy is often confused with being happy. The state of being happy is an emotional response. You can be happy and not have any joy. Joy on the other hand is the confidence, assurance, hope, trust and peace that we have in Jesus. Joy does not require a smile or laughter to appear on the outside. Joy comes from and dwells deep within our innermost being.

[105] The "you" is in a plural sense, more so than singular. God's work has been ongoing throughout the years and will continue throughout our lifetime, culminating at Jesus's second coming. How is God working through you and your daily activities?

Why was Paul joyful in spirit (v. 5)? _____

_____

Does God start something and then stop (v. 6)? _____

_____

When God gets through with me, I will come forth as what? _____

📖

"It is right for me to feel this way about all of you, since I have you in my heart; for whether I am in chains or defending and confirming the gospel, all of you share in God's grace with me. God can testify how I long for all of you with the affection of Christ Jesus" (vv. 7-8).

What is the result of carrying one in your heart (v. 7)? _____

_____

What is the exciting news about God's grace (v. 7)? _____

_____

How does God testify (v. 8)? _____

📖

"And this is my prayer[106]; that your love may abound more and more in knowledge and depth of insight" (v. 9).

What is Paul's prayer (vv. 9-11)?

1. _____
2. _____
3. _____
4. _____
5. _____
6. _____
7. _____

---

[106] When we pray, do we pray for others or just for self? When we pray for others, do we pray that they will continually gain wisdom? God has created us to be a fine tune instrument of love. And we should always strive to be polished through every aspect of our lives, especially in the service of Jesus Christ.

How do you abound more in knowledge? _____
_____

How do you abound in depth of insight? _____
_____

📖

"So that you may be able to discern what is best and may be pure and blameless until the day of Christ[107], filled with the fruit of righteousness that comes through Jesus Christ, to the glory and praise of God" (vv. 10-11).

We discern what is best according to the thought of whom (v. 10)? _____
_____

What can we do to make ourselves pure (v. 10)? _____
Can we be completely blameless (v. 10)? _____
_____

What is a one word term for "fruits of righteousness" (v. 11)? _____
The Christian personality originates from whom (v. 11)? _____

PROCLAMATION

"Now I want you to know, brothers that what has happen to me has really served to advance the gospel" (v. 12).

What can we do to proclaim the Gospel (v. 12)? _____
_____

Does a story always have to be about "good times"? _____
_____
_____

Silence in regards to the proclaiming the Gospel may denote what? _____
(Hint: Romans 1:15-17) _____
_____

---

[107] Pure and blameless are subsets of each other. You can't have one and not the other. The only one who is exactly both is Jesus himself. As we journey, our objective should be, to be like Jesus in our talk, thoughts and actions.

"As a result, it has become clear throughout the whole palace guard and to everyone else that I am in chains for Christ[108]. Because of my chains, most of the brothers in the Lord have been encouraged to speak the word of God more courageously and fearlessly" (vv. 13-14).

How do we recognize people that are of Christ (v. 13)? _____

_____

What is told to us about Paul's situation (v. 13)? _____

_____

What is the effect of telling the complete inhibited story (v. 14)? _____

_____

God is telling us in these verses to what (vv. 12-14)? _____
(Hint: 1 Peter 2:9) _____

_____

"It is true that some preach Christ out of envy and rivalry, but others out of goodwill. The latter do so in love, knowing that I am put here for the defense of the gospel. The former preach Christ out of selfish ambition[109], not sincerely, supposing that they can stir up trouble for me while I am in chains" (vv. 15-17).

Does everybody preach for the same reason (v. 15)? _____

_____

How do we know who preaches for the right reason (v. 16)? _____

_____

_____

[108] Paul loved Jesus so much that he was willing to devote his life to Jesus and take a stand for him. The question that comes today is, how deep is your love? Is it only found once per week or when trauma strikes? Or does it only appear when it draped across the eyes of society? Show you love for Jesus and devote yourself to Him.

[109] Selfish ambition is deceptive and detrimental. It encompasses the three narcissistic evils: me, myself and I. Success becomes an illusion when self is put first or is the underlying motive. The beginning and the end result of self-ambition is simply a pretense, a con.

Preaching out of envy and rivalry (strife) is also known as (v. 17)? _____

Preaching from self-ambition carries an under tone of what (v. 17)? _____

📖

"But what does it matter? The important thing is that in every way, whether from false motives or true, Christ is preached[110]. And because of this I rejoice" (v. 18).

Whether out of bad or good preaching, what is the result? _____

REAL LIVING

"For I know that through your prayers and the help given by the Spirit of Jesus Christ[111], what has happened to me will turn out for my deliverance" (v. 19).

Real living means that we walk with what? _____

We need what even though our intentions are good? _____

What is the good side of persecution and suffering for Christ? _____

As a Christian, what are some things that we should be ashamed of?
    1. _____

---

110   Time and time again, you hear in conversations that ministry over social media and the network is false, all of them just want money, and they have the wrong motive. Paul states that the motive is not something to worry about or even consider, because whether it is bad or good, the word of Jesus Christ is proclaimed.

111   Paul shows his confidence in the Holy Spirit, Jesus and His word. To "know" means to not have any doubt or question. There is a conviction of being convinced with expectation that what is to come will come to fruition by the power of God.

2. _____

3. _____

📖

"I eagerly expect and hope that I will in no way be ashamed[112], but will have sufficient courage so that now as always Christ will be exalted in my body, whether by life or by death" (v. 20).

What is Paul hoping that he will not be ashamed of? _____
_____

What is Paul telling us about prayer and God?

1. _____

2. _____

When should Christ be exalted? _____

📖

"For to me, to live is Christ and to die is gain[113]. If I am to go on living in the body, this will mean fruitful labor for me. Yet what shall I choose? I do not know" (vv. 21-22).

What does it mean "to live is Christ" (v. 21)? _____
_____

What does it mean "to die is gain" (v. 21)? _____
_____

---

[112] Some people are afraid to witness or show their faith in Jesus, because of the possible negative response. If we take the name of Jesus and invoke the power of the Holy Spirit, God will give us what we need, in the manner that we need, in order to obtain the result that God desires. So let us live without the fear, but with courage, knowing that God is with us and God is the conductor.

[113] Paul is arguing that life on this earth becomes wonderful (outside of the setbacks, disappointments, injustice and attacks) as we strive to be like Jesus and to live for Him. If we die, as Christians, we will be with Christ (no better place to be). Therefore, no matter the situation, if we have breath or not, it is a benefit for those who are in Christ Jesus.

How can labor be fruitful (v. 22)? _____

_____

📖

"I am torn between the two: I desire to depart and be with Christ, which is better by far, but it is more necessary for you that I remain in the body[114]" (vv. 23-24).

Why is there confusion for Paul (vv. 22-23)? _____

_____

Why is it more necessary/needful for Paul to remain in the body/flesh (v. 24)? _____

_____

What is your purpose here on earth?

1. _____
2. _____
3. _____
4. _____
5. _____

📖

"Convinced of this, I know that I will remain, and I will continue with all of you for your progress and joy in the faith, so that through my being with you again your joy in Christ Jesus will overflow on account of me" (vv. 25-26).

Like Paul, as believers, what should we be convinced or confident about (v. 25)? _____

_____

Is "joy of faith" or "joy in the faith" an emotional reaction (v. 25)? _____

_____

[114] Sometimes in our lives we come to crossroads where a decision has to be made. Paul wanted to be with Jesus, but he also knew that the people needed his leadership to help them mature in Christ. Thus, the choice became, do I benefit myself or do I reach out and help others. Paul helped himself by making the decision to reach out help someone else. What sacrifices are you making for others to benefit?

How can the joy in others overflow or be more abundant (v. 26)? _____

_____

SUFFERING

"Whatever happens, conduct yourselves in a manner worthy of the gospel of Christ[115]. Then, whether I come and see you or only hear about you in my absence, I will know that you stand firm in one spirit, contending as one man for the faith of the gospel without being frightened in anyway by those who oppose you. This is a sign to them that they will be destroyed, but that you will be saved and that by God" (vv. 27-28).

How should we conduct ourselves (v. 27)? _____

_____

To stand "firm" or "fast," our attitude must be what (v. 28)? _____

_____

What shall a man _____ in exchange for his _____
(Matthew 16:26)
Standing strong in Christ reveals what (v. 28)? _____

_____

📖

"For it has been granted to you on behalf of Christ not only to believe on Him, but also to suffer for Him, since you are going through the same struggle you saw I had, and now hear that I still have" (vv. 29-30).

What is the privilege that we have received as Christians (v. 29)? _____

_____

So _____ and _____
is a gift from God (v. 29)
How long will Christians suffer (v. 30)? _____

_____

---

[115] In our dealings with one another, whether inside the church or in the community, we need to be united in our faith, stand and service for Jesus. We must avoid strife, stirring up arguments and causing injury. Prayer must be our first weapon from start to finish with peace in Jesus as the prize.

PLEASURE FOUND IN SERVICE: PHILIPPIANS 2

CHAPTER BLUEPRINT

IMITATION

"If you have any encouragement from being united with Christ[116], if any comfort from His love, if any fellowship with the Spirit, if any tenderness and compassion" (v. 1).

Because the sentence starts with the word "If," then one may induce what? _____

_____

God is telling us that as Christians we should what?

_____

---

[116] Paul starts off this Chapter with 5 conditions, emphasized with the word "If." If you meet the condition than a result will follow. This also raises eyebrows to the knowledge that there are Christians without these characteristics or experiences. And if this is true, then it is possible that some people have confess Jesus as Lord for self-ambition or social status or inclusiveness or possibly out of obligation or guilt. In any of these cases, the belief or confession may not have been authentic. One could possibly sum up these conditions in the definition and exhibit of "joy." Are these conditions present or missing in your life?

1. _____
2. _____
3. _____
4. _____
5. _____

How are we encouraged by being with Christ? _____

_____

How does God's love comfort us? _____

_____

What are we supposed to do regarding the Holy Spirit? _____

_____

What is meant by compassion or bowels? _____

_____

What is meant by tenderness or mercies? _____

_____

📖

"Then make my joy complete by being like-minded, having the same love, being one in spirit and purpose[117]" (v. 2).

What are Christians called to do?

1. _____
2. _____
3. _____
4. _____

📖

"Do nothing out of selfish ambition or vain conceit[118], but in humility consider others better than yourselves" (v. 3).

---

[117] In order for joy to be complete, joy should manifest itself with these four results, which germinated in the five conditions in the previous verse.

[118] Society sometimes think that people who go to church all go for the same reason. The church is very diverse with cultures, motives, genders, talents and gifts. Scripture has shown us that some people come for personal edification and benefits. We shouldn't be shocked if we find such a person. Instead, we need to be humble. We should continually pray that the Holy Spirit may intervene, and

What was a problem with the church in Philippi? _____

How do we consider others?

1. _____
2. _____

📖

"Each of you should look not only to your own interests, but also to the interests of others. Your attitude should be the same as that of Christ Jesus[119]" (vv. 4-5).

What should you look to (v. 4)? _____

Your attitude should be what (v. 5)? _____

EXALTATION

"Who, being in very nature God, did not consider equality with God something to be grasped, but made Himself nothing, taking the very nature of a servant, being made in human likeness" (vv. 6-7).

How is Christ the "very form" or "very nature" of God (v. 6)? _____

How long has Jesus existed? _____

How was Jesus equal to God (v. 6)? _____

In order to be an example of the Lord, it may require what (v. 7)? _____

---

pray that our perception and actions are accepting in love, bringing unity, not discrimination or abuse.

[119] This verse, like so many others, exhibits the humanity of Jesus, both God and man. Throughout scripture, believers are called to renew their mind in order to be like Christ. Believers have to make an effort to alter their thinking to that of holiness in order to obtain the right results. Followers have to spend time in studying, meditating and praying in God's word night and day. It is not enough just to go to church once or twice a week. It helps, but, a person can be defined by the manner in which they think.

📖

"And being found in appearance as a man[120], He humbled Himself and became obedient to death[121], even death on a cross" (v. 8).

Once God was found what did Jesus do? _____
_____

As believers in Christ, we are to what? _____
How long should we be obedient? _____

📖

"Therefore God exalted Him to the highest place and gave Him the name that is above every name[122]" (v. 9).

Where did God exalt Jesus? _____
What is the name that is above every name? _____
How is the name Jesus superior to others? _____
_____

📖

"That at the name of Jesus every knee should bow, in heaven and on earth and under the earth" (v.10)

Bowing down on your knees symbolizes what?

1. _____
2. _____
3. _____
4. _____

---

[120] Jesus was fully God who revealed himself to humanity in the likeness of man with all consequences.

[121] Humble and meek can be interchanged as synonyms of each other in meaning. God is displaying through Jesus, that pride has no place in the kingdom of God. Make up in your mind today, that you will follow the teachings of Jesus until your last breath, regardless of your situation or who is supporting you.

[122] God is the creator of heaven and earth. True rewards come from God. There is no pretense or ulterior motive with God. In your living, look to God to lift or promote you or give you the increase. Joshua is the Hebrew name for Jesus, which means "He saves."

5. _____

Who will all bow? _____

📖

"And every tongue confess that Jesus Christ is Lord[123], to the glory of God the Father" (v. 11).

What will be confessed? _____
What does Lord mean? _____
_____
_____

Confession will be made to the glory of whom? _____

LIGHTS AND STARS

"Therefore, my dear friends, as you have always obeyed, not only in my presence, but now much more in my absence, continue to work out your salvation with fear and trembling, for it is God who works in you to will and to act according to His good purpose" (vv. 12-13).

Who is Paul talking to (v. 12)? _____
When should we obey God (v. 12)? _____
_____

What is meant by "work out your own salvation" (v. 12)? _____
_____
_____

"fear' and "trembling" refers to what (v. 12)? _____
_____

We are obedient to God because of what (v. 13)? _____
_____
_____

---

[123] Confession is a means which one makes known what is truly in the heart.

📖

"Do everything without complaining and arguing[124]" (v. 14).

Do everything without _____
and _____
Why do people in general complain argue about things? _____
_____

📖

"So that you may become blameless and pure children of God[125], without fault in a crooked and depraved generation[126], in which you shine like stars in the universe as you hold out the word of life[127], in order that I may boast on the day of Christ that I did not run or labor for nothing" (vv. 15-16).

Why should we not argue and complain (v. 15)?
1. _____
2. _____
3. _____

What is the difference between blameless and pure (harmless) (v. 15)? ___
_____

Why do "true" Christians shine like stars (vv. 15-16)? _____
_____

To "hold out" or to "hold forth" means what (v. 16)? _____

---

[124] One of the hardest things to do is go through life without expressing our thoughts, hurts, disappointments or disagreements. But if one is operating in the power of the Holy Spirit, then love and appreciation will be the instrument that initiates and keeps the peace.

[125] When you are blamed, the finger is pointed at you for not taking responsibility or accountability. Your life should be one of truth, innocence and not guilty.

[126] Dishonesty, crime, injustice, oppression, discrimination, racism, bigotry, and alienation to name a few are all around us. It can be found at work, home, school, church, and government. As a Christian, you do not have a choice. You must give every effort in the name of Jesus, to rise above at all times.

[127] The word of life is God's plan of salvation to all mankind that will listen and believe. When you accept Jesus Christ as Lord and Savior, your life now belongs to Him, and not in the same manner as the world.

When is the "day of Christ" (v. 16)? _____

What will you boast about when questioned by Jesus (v. 16)? _____
_____

📖

"But even if I am being poured out like a drink offering on the sacrifice and service coming from your faith, I am glad and rejoice with all of you. So you too should be glad and rejoice with me" (vv. 17-18).

Our attitude should be what when our life is sacrificed for someone else (vv. 17-18)? _____

In order to shine like lights or stars, our lives need to be ordered like? ___
_____

TIMOTHY AND EPAPHRODITUS

"I hope in the Lord Jesus to send Timothy to you soon, that I also may be cheered when I receive news about you. I have no else like him, who takes a genuine interest in your welfare" (vv. 19-20).

What do we know about Timothy (v. 19)?
   1. _____
   2. _____
   3. _____
   4. _____

What is the point of continuing to send someone to the church (v. 19)? _
_____
   1. _____ Hint: Reinforce_____
   2. _____ Hint: Communication_____

Open communication may give rise to what emotion (v. 19)? _____
What was one of the problems in the church (v. 20)? _____
_____

A lack of hospitality reflects a lack of what (v. 20)? _____

_____

📖

"For everyone looks out for his own interests, not those of Jesus Christ[128]"
(v.21).

What was another problem in the church? _____

_____

Churches have problems when in all areas when? _____

_____

The workers are many, but the laborers are? _____

📖

"But you know that Timothy has proved himself[129], because as a son with
his father he has served with me in the work of the gospel" (v. 22).

What is Paul reminding the church about Timothy? _____

_____

Do we recruit people and do people respond the same way they did in the
past? _____

_____

📖

"I hope, therefore, to send him as soon as I see how things go with me.
And I am confident in the Lord that I myself will come soon" (vv. 23-24).

Once we have trained a person, do we let them go? _____

_____

---

[128] To look out for the interest of Jesus means we have to spend time with Jesus on
a regular basis. Our mind and attitude must be at a level of surrender to Him
for His will, God's will to be done.

[129] It has been said that faith in Jesus without it showing in your daily activities is
worthless. What are you displaying and proving to your heavenly Father?

📖

"But I think it is necessary to send back to you Epaphroditus, my brother, fellow worker and fellow soldier, who is also your messenger, whom you sent to take care of my needs. For he longs for all of you and is distressed because you heard he was ill[130]. In deed he was ill, and almost died. But God had mercy on him, and not on him only but also on me, to spare me sorrow upon sorrow" (vv. 25-27).

What do we know about Epaphroditus (vv. 25-26)?

1. _____
2. _____
3. _____
4. _____
5. _____
6. _____

What happened to Epaphroditus (vv. 26-27)? _____

What did God do for Epaphroditus (v. 27)? (Hint: Exodus 23:25) _____

_____

Why was Paul so eager to send Epaphroditus? _____

_____

📖

"Therefore I am all the more eager to send him, so that when you see him again you may be glad and I may have less anxiety" (v. 28).

Is taking care of ill adults easy? _____

_____

📖

"Welcome him in the Lord with great joy and honor men like him, because he almost died for the work of Christ, risking his life to make up for the help you could not give me" (vv. 29-30).

---

[130]   To be distressed in this case means to be bothered or troubled to the point of being in pain. This is not to be confused with physical pain, but it is the pain that comes from worry.

What should you do with God's messengers (vv. 29-30)?

1. _____
2. _____
3. _____

Why should you give such people of God this special treatment? _____
_____

BENEFITS OF BELIEF: PHILIPPIANS 3

CHAPTER BLUEPRINT
- Flesh is Inadequate   (3:1 – 3:11)
- Pressing Toward the Goal   (3:12 – 3:16)
- Our Citizenship   (3:17 – 3:21)

FLESH IS INADEQUATE

"Finally, my brothers, rejoice in the Lord[131]! It is no trouble for me to write the same things to you again, and it is a safeguard for you" (v.1).

What are Christians supposed to do no matter what? _____

_____

What is safe or a safeguard? _____

_____

📖

"Watch out for those dogs, those men who do evil, those mutilators of the flesh" (v.2).

What type of people should Christians be on guard?
1. _____
2. _____

---

[131] When we think about the Lord, what He has done and what He is doing, our joy should boil over in happiness, praise and thanksgiving, day and night throughout each and every year.

3. _____

Who were considered the dogs or evil men in Paul's day? _____
_____

📖

"For it is we who are the circumcision[132], we who worship by the Spirit of God, who glory in Christ Jesus, and who put no confidence in the flesh, though I myself have reasons for such confidence" (vv. 3-4).

Who are the circumcised (v. 3)? _____
_____

How Christians are supposed to worship (v. 3)? _____
_____

What are four distinguishing characteristics of true Christians (v. 3)?

    1. _____

    2. _____

    3. _____

    4. _____

Why does Paul feel that he has more reasons to put confidence in flesh (v. 4)? _____
_____

📖

"Circumcised on the eight day, of the people of Israel, of the tribe of Benjamin, a Hebrew of Hebrews; in regards to the law, a Pharisee[133]; as

---

[132] Circumcision was a Jewish rite or practice that was exercised on males in accordance to the law. It was a symbol that those who received this rite belonged to the family of God. The true believers in Jesus Christ are God's family, and are the circumcised.

[133] A Pharisee was a well-educated leader and member of the Jewish group or sect that adhered to, and interpret the written and traditional Old Testament laws. They were political, but not to the point of the Sadducees. For the most part, they believed in the resurrection of the dead. However, they were against Jesus

for zeal, persecuting the church; as for legalistic righteousness, faultless" (vv. 5-6).

What is the significance of being circumcised on the eighth day (v.5)? ___
_____

Why the tribe of Benjamin is mentioned (v.5)? _____
_____

What is the correlation between law and Pharisee (v.5)? _____
_____

What is legalistic righteousness (v.6)? _____
_____
_____

📖

"But whatever was to my profit I now consider loss for the sake of Christ" (v.7).

Why Paul's profit is considered a loss? _____
_____
_____

📖

"What is more, I consider everything a loss compared to the surpassing greatness of knowing Christ Jesus my Lord, for whose sake I have lost all things. I consider them rubbish, that I may gain Christ and be found in Him, not having a righteousness of my own that comes from the law, but that which is through faith in Christ, the righteousness that comes from God and is by faith" (vv. 8-9).

Compared to knowing Christ, how does everything else measure up (v. 8)? _____
_____

What is the cost of following Jesus wholeheartedly (v. 8)? _____
_____

because Christ exposed their inner intentions in their heart and daily activities, whether, spiritual or social.

What is the point of considering everything meaningless (vv. 8-9)?

1. _____

2. _____

Real righteousness comes from whom (v. 9)? _____

📖

"I want to know Christ and the power of His resurrection and the fellowship of sharing in His sufferings[134], becoming like Him in His death[135], and so, somehow, to attain to the resurrection from the dead" (v. 10).

As Christians, as believers, we should all seek what?

1. _____

2. _____

3. _____

4. _____

5. _____

PRESSING TOWARD THE GOAL

"Not that I have already obtained all this, or have already been made perfect, but I press on to take hold of that for which Christ Jesus took hold of me" (v. 12).

What type of attitude is Paul displaying? _____
_____

Paul is telling us that our goal as believers should be what? _____
_____
_____

---

[134] The power spoken here has had a couple of interpretations. 1. Some believe that Paul is talking about the power of the actual resurrection of Christ that took place only one time. 2. Power could mean the Holy Spirit that operates in the daily lives of believers, and is their instrument for strength and path.

[135] What are your motives for believing in Jesus? Is it out of distress, loss, defeat, disappointment, hurt or is it out of love, reverence and appreciation? Something to think about is, how far are you willing to go to know Christ, share in His suffering, His death and resurrection?

📖

"Brothers, I do not consider myself yet to have taken hold of it. But one thing I do: Forgetting what is behind and straining toward what is ahead[136], I press on toward the goal to win the prize for which God has called me heavenward in Christ Jesus" (vv. 13-14).

In order to take hold of God, you must do what (v. 13)?

1. _____
2. _____

Is Paul telling us to forget our past (v. 13)? _____
_____

What types of things are Christians supposed to be reaching for (v. 13)? _
_____

To "press" means what (v. 14)? _____
_____

What is the "prize" that Christians are seeking (v. 14)? _____
_____
_____

📖

"All of us who are mature should take such a view of things[137]. And if on some point you think differently, that too God will make clear to you" (v.15).

Mature believers should see their life in what kind of light? _____
_____

How does God reveal or make clear to believers His plan? _____

---

[136] How often do we forget? As Christians, the exercise of forgetting and not placing it on the table or agenda is an ongoing thing. Why? Because we are constantly faced with trials and elements that could be a hindrance to our spiritual growth. Whether good or bad, the past is the past, and therefore cannot be changed. Live today in Jesus and look for tomorrow in Christ.

[137] Mature is referring to the believers who not only have accepted Jesus as their Savior, but to those who make every effort to live a life that is holy and pleasing to God in Christ Jesus. Their growth is exhibit in a state of righteousness that is not of their own, but is in the righteousness that comes from God.

📖

"Only let us live up to what we have already attained" (v. 16).

Live up to what we have obtained means what? _____
_____
_____

OUR CITIZENSHIP

"Join with others in following my example, brothers, and take note of those who live according to the pattern we gave you[138]" (v. 17).

Who should believers join in with? _____
_____

To "note" or to "take note" means what? _____
_____

📖

"For, as I have often told you before and now say again even with tears, many live as enemies of the cross of Christ" (v.18).

What is causing Paul to weep or cry? _____
_____

If many are enemies of Christ, why does mankind look for acceptance among men? _____
_____

---

[138] A pattern is not only a road map, but it is a copy or duplicate of an original element. Paul is referring the life style of righteousness of God that has been taught and shown. The life style that you are portraying, is it positive pattern for others to emulate or copy?

📖

"Their destiny is destruction, their god is their stomach, and their glory is in their shame. Their mind is on earthly things[139]" (v.19).

What are the rewards of the enemies of Christ?

1. _____
2. _____
3. _____

The mindset of the enemy is on what? _____

📖

"But our citizenship is in heaven. And we eagerly await a Savior from there, the Lord Jesus Christ, who, by the power that enables Him to bring everything under His control, will transform our lowly bodies so that they will be like His glorious body[140]" (vv. 20-21).

As Believers, as Christians, where is our citizenship (v. 20)? _____

_____

When comparing to earthly things, why does Paul mention the citizenship of believers (v. 20)? _____

_____

What should you as a Christian be valuing?

1. _____
2. _____
3. _____
4. _____
5. _____

---

[139] Destiny sometimes means the end. In this verse, destiny can be defined as the purpose or calling. When someone feels pulled to a particular activity, we classify and verbalize it as a calling (i.e., ministry) or purpose. What is the voice of destiny that speaks within you?

[140] Lowly bodies does not mean that God created bodies that are average or less than par. It means that the bodies that we currently have are for the life here on earth as we know it, and are subject to the conditions thereof. When Jesus transforms are bodies, it will be without disabilities, pain, suffering, injury, hunger, and it will be magnificent, outstanding and superb like His.

6. _____

7. _____

8. _____

9. _____

10. _____

Who or what is the power or workings (v. 21)? _____

What will Jesus do (v. 21)? _____

_____

In summary Paul is telling us to rejoice because? _____

_____

_____

ADVANTAGE OF GIVING: PHILIPPIANS 4

CHAPTER BLUEPRINT

- Be Steadfast   (4:1)
- Be United   (4:2 – 4:7)
- Think on These   (4:8 – 4:9)
- Charity   (4:10 – 4:20)
- Greeting   (4:21 – 4:23)

BE STEADFAST

"Therefore, my brothers, you whom I love and long for, my joy and crown that is how you should stand firm in the Lord, dear friends!" (v. 1).

How can your brothers and sisters be your joy and crown? _____
_____

How do you stand firm or steadfast? _____
_____

BE UNITED

"I plead with Euodia and I plead with Syntyche to agree with each other in the Lord" (v. 2).

Who are Euodia and Syntyche? _____

What is the problem with these two people? _____

📖

"Yes, and I ask you, loyal yokefellow, help these women who have contended at my side in the cause of the gospel, along with Clement and the rest of my fellow workers[141], whose names are in the book of life" (v. 3).

Who is the loyal yokefellow or true companion? _____
What is the Book of Life? _____

Who are the names in the book of life? _____
What are members of the church called to do? _____

📖

"Rejoice in the Lord always[142]. I will say it again: Rejoice!" (v. 4).

What are all Christians called to do? _____

📖

"Let your gentleness be evident to all[143]. The Lord is near" (v. 5).

---

[141] Fame is an element of this world. Our value does not come from this world but our value comes from who we are in God according to God's eyes. Therefore, when it states "fellow workers," it is understood that it is not always necessary to have each of our names mentioned. We don't have to worry about the world clinging to and remembering our names. We can relax, because God knows who we are, and our reward comes from Him.

[142] Rejoicing in the Lord should be a regular activity on the same level as taking a breath. When pondering about the goodness of the Lord, all the things God has brought you through and how Jesus has made a way of salvation, and has placed your feet on solid ground; your joy and happiness should be exploding with praise and adoration.

[143] When one is gentle, the treatment of others in a kind, respectable, fair and tender manner is exercised. This may include being slow to speak, and making sure that the tone of speech low and calm, and is free from injustice and injury.

Through what means are Christians to rejoice? _____
_____

Your gentleness should be known by whom? _____
_____

What does this verse infer about revenge? _____
_____

What does this verse infer about personal rights? _____
_____

The Lord is near or at hand means what? _____
_____

📖

"Do not be anxious about anything, but in everything, by prayer and petition, with thanksgiving, present your requests to God[144]" (v. 6).

To be anxious means what? _____
_____

What are some things that you should worry about? _____
_____

How are you to present your request to God?
   1. _____
     Which means? _____
   2. _____
     Which means? _____
   3. _____
     Which means? _____

---

[144] The world that we live in emphasizes speed. Everything that we do must be performed in faster and faster times according to the standards of the world. Technology is constantly finding ways to speed progress. Science is now defining and classifying things according to rate and speed (i.e., cooking, travel, education, etc.). One problem that appears to exist is that when we ask of God, we ask with expectations for immediate response and without sincere thanksgiving. Don't be in a rush. Take time to show God your gratitude, and let your asking be guided by the Holy Spirit, whereby Jesus and God's will is lifted up.

To "present" or "let" or "make" illustrates what personality characteristic?

_____

What should we go to God for? _____

_____

📖

"And the peace of God, which transcends all understanding[145], will guard your hearts and your minds in Christ Jesus" (v. 7).

How is the Peace of God found in positive thinking? _____

_____

How is the Peace of God found in the absence of disagreement? _____

_____

What understanding is Paul talking about? _____

_____

God's peace protects what? _____

_____

Explain how God's peace protects or doesn't protect your body? _____

_____

Think on These

"Finally, brothers, whatever is true, whatever is noble[146], whatever is right, whatever is pure, whatever is lovely, whatever is admirable, if anything is excellent or praiseworthy, think about such things" (v. 8).

It is not what goes in the mouth that defiles a man, but what (Matt. 15:11)? _____

What we contribute determines what? _____

_____

How do you replace harmful input in your mind? _____

---

[145] To transcend or surpass means to go beyond the normal boundaries or limits with no establishment of new restrictions.

[146] Noble is a synonym for honorable. Are the activities and words of your mouth something to be shameful of or do they display a character of high morals and a speech seasoned with salt?

What does God say that we are to think about?

1. _____
   Which are: _____

2. _____
   Which are: _____

3. _____
   Which are: _____

4. _____
   Which are: _____

5. _____
   Which are: _____

6. _____
   Which are: _____

7. _____
   Which are: _____

8. _____
   Which are: _____

📖

"Whatever you have learned or received or heard from me, or seen in me, put it into practice[147]. And the God of peace will be with you" (v. 9).

What should you put into practice?

1. _____
From where? _____

2. _____
From what? _____

3. _____
From whom? _____

4. _____
Perceive what? _____

---

[147] If one hears the word and does not exercise what has been received, then what good is it? In order for change and growth to take place, it is paramount that we give every effort to exercise or do what we have learned.

A person performs in the manner that they what? _____

What will be with you? _____

_____

CHARITY

"I rejoice greatly in the Lord that at last you have received your concern for me. Indeed, you have been concerned, but you had no opportunity to show it[148]. I am not saying this because I am in need, for I have learned to be content whatever the circumstances[149]" (vv. 10-11).

Paul is happy because of what (v. 10)? _____

_____

Happiness can be brought to others by means of what? _____

_____

If we become bogged down with life, what should we do about others (v. 10)? _____

_____

To be "content" means what (v. 11)? _____

_____

---

[148] It is good to have some uneasiness when it comes to certain things. The church had thoughts and worries in regards to the level of support that was being shared with those of the ministry, but previously did not reveal it. Concern, worries, anxiety or mixed thoughts need to be brought to the surface where it can be addressed and resolved for the sake of peace and wholeness.

[149] Stoic philosophy sees a contented person as one who accepts no matter the circumstance. And in Greek philosophy, this word represented self-sufficiency. Others have claimed it is when one is in a state of relaxation. The person is comfortable and satisfied. When we are able to view and appreciate life through the standards of the Lord, when our minds and hearts are open to God, then we are able to understand God's perspective of life. This appears to be easy when things are going the way that we expect. But when life is not as sunny as we like, are we fulfilled with what we have? Are we pleased about where when have been and what we have been through? Does the result of our contentment place us in an emotional state of calmness? Yes should be our answer for all situations.

📖

"I know what it is to be in need, and I know what it is to have plenty. I have learned the secret of being content in any and every situation, whether well fed or hungry, whether living in plenty or in want. I can do everything through Him who gives me strength" (vv. 12-13).

Verse 12 confirms what philosophical definition of content (v. 12)? _____

What are the things that we can do (v. 13)? _____
_____

📖

"Yet it was good of you to share in my troubles. Moreover, as you Philippians know, in the early days of your acquaintance with the gospel, when I set out from Macedonia, not one church shared with me in the manner of giving and receiving, except you only; for even when I was in Thessalonica, you sent me aid again and again when I was in need" (vv. 14-16).

While Paul was in prison what did the Philippians do (v. 14)? _____
Verse 14 is explained how (vv. 15-16)? _____
_____

📖

"Not that I am looking for a gift[150], but I am looking for what may be credited to your account"
    (v. 17).

What is credited to us when we give? _____
_____

---

[150] It is good to lift up what builds up the character of another, as well as, for self. Christians must be careful that the acts or deeds that are performed are exercised for the right reason and purpose. If our giving and/or serving is based on receiving a reward of some kind, then our mission and intent needs to be checked, and placed back in alignment with God's word.

📖

"I have received full payment and even more; I am amply supplied, now that I have received from Epaphroditus the gifts you sent. They are a fragrant offering[151], an acceptable sacrifice, pleasing to God" (v. 18).

Who is Epaphroditus? _____

_____

What was the gift that Paul received? _____

How should our gifts to others be described?

    1. _____

    2. _____

    3. _____

📖

"And my God will meet all your needs according to His glorious riches in Christ Jesus[152]" (v. 19).

What will God do? _____

_____

What could be a problem in the interpretation of this verse? _____

_____

📖

"To our God and Father be glory forever and ever. Amen" (v. 20).

When we realize all what God has done, doing and will do, our response is what? _____

_____

---

[151] A flagrant offering is a type of fellowship offering that expresses thanksgiving and adoration to the Lord.

[152] It is the most wonderful thing to know that God will meet all of our needs. Needs should not be confused with desires. Desires can originate from the flesh and may not be in our best interest. However, God knows what is best for us, and He willing gives and satisfies of His name sake.

GREETING

"Greet all the saints in Christ Jesus. The brothers who are with me send greetings. All the saints send you greetings, especially those who belong to Caesar's household" (vv. 21-22).

What should Christians do (v. 21)? _____
_____

In some situations, people have a tendency to greet who? _____
_____

The Bible is applicable for everyday life for generations to come because people have what? _____
Our greetings should extend to whom (v. 21-22)? _____
_____

📖

"The grace of the Lord Jesus Christ be with your spirit. Amen" (v. 23).

Our blessing in the beginning and end should be what (v. 2 & 23)? _____
_____

Colossians

1

Who is the Author: _____

When was the book written (B.C., A.D): _____

From what location was the book written? _____

What number is the book in the New Testament: _____

What number is the book in Canonical Bible: _____

Setting or Location: _____

_____

What group of bodies in this letter written to? _____

What type of teaching was around the church that caused confusion among Christians? _____

_____

Certain members were promoting observance to Jewish rules and customs. Mysticism and false doctrines (which was heretical) during the early years proclaim that Jesus was a great teacher and Jesus was a higher being, but yet Jesus was not God. Pau is the epitome of apologetics. For Paul argues the Deity of Christ.

As believers in Christ, we are called to mature in our belief. This letter to the church of Colossae was written around the same time as that to the church of Ephesus, but with the theological thought that Christ can be found in believers.

BOOK BLUEPRINT

- The preeminence of Christ: Chapters 1 – 2
- The Christian Response: Chapters 3 - 4

MAJOR ARGUMENTS

Who is Jesus Christ? Jesus is God. When we think about the ultimate strength and power, known and unknown to mankind, the Almighty comes to mind whose name is Jesus. Jesus is sovereign and Jesus is complete. There is no one or no name that is above Him or holds more power than Jesus. Jesus existed before the beginning of time and He is Lord of all creation. This truth finds validity because Jesus, the Anointed One (Christ) is actually the incarnate God (God in the flesh).

Man's relationship with God has been separated through the acts of humanity embracing sin and the life that is in opposition of God. Because of the unselfish and loving acts of our Lord and Savior, we have been brought back, reconciled, united or connected to God by Jesus Christ through the forgiveness of sins. Our lives now identify and participate in the death, burial and resurrection of Jesus.

One of the problems of the Church is that it has a habit of appropriating the values and laws of society, incorporating the rules into the church, the Christian faith and making precedence therein. False leaders and teachers were discovered among the body of believers pressing a heresy that emphasized legalism, man or self-made rules.

The church was founded on the cornerstone, which became the capstone or chief. The cornerstone is Jesus himself. To recognize and to honor and obey Christ as the head of the church means that our loyalty is to Him. This loyalty must be welcomed, accepted, and grounded in all work and leadership that we perform and give thought.

CHRIST IS SOVEREIGN: COLOSSIANS 1

CHAPTER BLUEPRINT

GREETING

"Paul, an apostle of Christ Jesus by the will of God[153], and Timothy our brother. To the holy and faithful brothers in Christ at Colosse[154]: Grace and peace to you from God our Father" (vv.1-2).

---

[153] An Apostle was a messenger sent out to the world by Jesus to preach, heal those who were sick and cast out demons. The backgrounds of each varied. Thus, some people think that the 12 apostles represents the twelve tribes. Paul was no exception. His past history was not considered loving as he went around the land persecuting Believers. In any case, by God utilizing Paul as a messenger, we learn that God will use the gifts and talents that he has bestowed upon mankind that are willing to believe and follow Jesus. No matter what your history has been, God has a plan and place for you in His ministry.

[154] Colosse, just like Philippi, was located north of Ephesus. Different from Philippi, the habitation of Colosse carried a large population of Jews. There were beliefs of various kinds (which could be considered heretical) that were in conflict with the truth of the gospel.

How is Paul an apostle (v.1)? _____
_____

Who is the greeting address to (v. 2)? _____
_____

Is this different from the previous letters of Paul? _____
What is the problem in Colossae (v. 2)? _____
_____

THANKSGIVING AND PRAYER

"We always thank God, the Father of our Lord Jesus Christ[155], when we pray for you, because we have heard of your faith in Christ Jesus and of the love you have for all the saints" (vv. 3-4).

When you pray for others, what should you do (v. 3)? _____
What do we need to do in order to truly thank God for others (v. 4)? ___
_____

What did Paul noticed in other believers (v. 4)? _____
_____

"The faith and love that spring from the hope that is stored up for you in heaven and that you have already heard about in the word of truth, the gospel that has come to you. All over the world this gospel is bearing fruit and growing, just as it has been doing among you since the day you heard it and understood God's grace in all its truth[156]" (vv. 5-6).

Hope is stored where (v. 5)? _____

---

[155] Giving thanks and appreciation is an activity that keeps a believer humble and without self-ambition. When we pray, it is good to give reverence to God, who gives us the ability and opportunity for all things.

[156] Grace is that unwarranted, unearned favor that only comes from God, who He willingly extends to believers. Through the grace of God, people have the opportunity to hear the message of truth, be delivered from their ways, and transformed in their thinking, to have a mind like Christ, and live a life more plentiful.

Hope is the result of what (v. 5)? _____

_____

How does Gnosticism and the Gospel differ (v. 6)? _____

_____

When did the movement of the Gospel start (v. 6)? _____

_____

📖

"You learned it from Epaphras[157], our dear fellow servant, who is a faithful minister of Christ on our behalf, and who also told us of your love in the Spirit" (vv. 7-8).

Who is Epaphras (vv. 7-8)?
    1. _____
    2. _____
    3. _____
    4. _____

How a church of the Gospel is generally planted? _____

_____

What is love in the Spirit (v.8)? _____

_____

INCOMPARABILITY OF CHRIST

"For this reason, since the day we heard about you we have not stopped praying for you and asking God to fill you with the knowledge of His will through all spiritual wisdom and understanding" (v. 9)

What is the reason Paul and fellow servants have been praying? _____

_____

The same activity was expressed in Ephesians 1:15. What does this infer about our prayer life? _____

_____

---

[157] This person is recognized as minister of the word of Christ who help establish the church in Colosse.

What should be the petition of our prayer? _____
_____

"And we pray this in order that you may live a life worthy of the Lord and may please Him in every way[158]: bearing fruit in every good work, growing in the knowledge of God, being strengthen with all power according to His glorious might so that you may have great endurance and patience, and joyfully giving thanks to the Father, who has qualified you to share in the inheritance of the saints in the kingdom of light[159]" (vv.10-12).

What is the motive behind Paul's prayer (v.10)?
1. _____
2. _____

How do we please God (vv. 10-12)?
1. _____
2. _____
3. _____
4. _____
5. _____

"For He has rescued us from the dominion of darkness and brought us into the kingdom of the Son He loves, in whom we have redemption, the forgiveness of sins[160]" (vv. 13-14).

---

[158] So many times are energy and efforts go to waste because we spend the energy in activities that give praise and kudos to man. The church is guilty of this when we placed all our trust in the leader instead of God. Remember, the leader, the pastor, the director are only instruments and messengers of God. Our adoration, honor and glory should be extended to God, and God only.

[159] How do you display your perseverance when things are not going your way, and difficulties are awaiting for you? When you trust in the Lord, He will give you the strength and the patience by the power of the Holy Spirit, that will result in a closer walk with Jesus, successful results, and a confidence that cannot be shaken. Be slow to react, and trust God to see you through.

[160] Rescued implies that a person may be in a situation where he has no control and the situation is keeping the person bound. Thus, the person needs to be

What are the powers or forces or dominion of darkness (v. 13)? _____

What is the kingdom (v. 13)? _____

What is the good news about the Son (v. 14)? _____
_____

GREATNESS OF CHRIST

"He is the image of the invisible God, the firstborn over all creation" (v.15).

Jesus is the image of who? _____
If God is the invisible God, then who is the visible God? _____
Being the firstborn means what? _____
_____

📖

"For by Him all things were created[161]: things in heaven and on earth, visible and invisible whether thrones or powers or rulers or authorities, all things were created by Him and for Him. He is before all things, and in Him all things hold together" (vv. 16-17).

What things were created by Jesus (v.16)?

    1. _____
    2. _____
    3. _____
    4. _____

---

delivered from their present state. Are there areas in your life where you feel bound and see no escape? Call on Jesus, who has the power to deliver no matter the circumstance.

[161] There are some people who think that matter is evil. They see earth and all creation as being evil. They also view God as completely good, and evil cannot come from good. Therefore, they reject the truth that God created the heavens and the earth. Paul is correcting this fallacy by informing that Jesus, God himself is the true and sole creator, which emphasizes the greatness or supremacy of Jesus.

5. _____
6. _____

When did Jesus actually come into existence (v. 17)? _____
All things in Him "consists" or "hold together" means what (v. 17)? ____
_____

📖

"And He is the head of the body, the church; He is the beginning and the firstborn from among the dead, so that in everything He might have the supremacy" (v. 18).

Jesus is the head of what? _____
How is Jesus the firstborn of the dead? _____
_____

RECONCILIATION

"For God was pleased to have all His fullness dwell in Him[162], and through Him to reconcile to himself all things, whether things on earth or things in heaven, by making peace through His blood, shed on the cross" (vv. 19-20).

The fullness of God that is available to us (Galatians 3:19) dwells where (v. 19)? _____
_____

What did the blood that was shed on the cross do (v. 20)? _____
_____

📖

"Once you were alienated from God and were enemies in your minds because of your evil behavior" (v.21).

---

[162] Fullness refers to Christ being human and divine at the same time. There were some (Gnostics) who believed that Christ was an entity that was above mankind but below heaven or God. Jesus has been before the existence of time and creation. Jesus is, has, and forever will be God. Therefore, when you have Jesus operating in your life, you have God operating in your life.

How are people and enemies alienated from God? _____

_____

When we are alienated from God, we become unknown or what? _____

"But now He has reconciled you by Christ's physical body through death to present you holy in His sight[163], without blemish and free from accusation if you continue in your faith, established and firm, not moved from the hope held out in the gospel. This is the gospel that you heard and that has been proclaimed to every creature under heaven, and of which I, Paul, have become a servant" (vv. 22-23).

How was atonement for our sins made so that we were presented as holy (v. 22)? _____

What is the condition of being reconciled by Christ (v. 23)? _____

_____

What is the "hope of the Gospel" (v. 23)? _____
Salvation has been proclaimed to who (v. 23)? _____

_____

SERVICE FOR THE CHURCH

"Now I rejoice in what was suffered for you, and I fill up in my flesh what is still lacking in regard to Christ's afflictions[164], for the sake of His body, which is the church" (v. 24).

---

[163] To be reconcile is to be reunited. Sin has separated man from God. Through the work of Jesus and the cross, man can now be brought back into a relationship with God through Christ Jesus by the power of the Holy Spirit. When reviewing your life, are you reconciled with God or are you trying to maneuver through life under your own power and sight? Is your flesh controlling your actions or is it Jesus?

[164] Paul is not talking about that the suffering Christ endured was inadequate. Paul was making the point that all believers and followers of Christ will face persecution and suffering. And this is something not to be down or depressed about because of fear, pain and hurt. God's will is being done through the

What suffering is Paul rejoicing about? _____
_____

What is meant by the "lacking in the affliction of Christ"? _____
_____

📖

"I have become its servant by the commission God gave me to present to you the word of God in its fullness, the mystery that has been kept hidden for ages and generations[165], but is now disclosed to the saints" (vv. 25-26).

Paul claims to be a minister or servant of what (v. 25)? _____
_____

The authority to proclaim or present the word of God comes from (v. 25)? _____

To present the "fullness" of God's Word means what (v. 26)? _____
_____

What is the mystery that had been kept hidden (v. 26)? _____
_____

The mystery is disclosed to who (v. 26)? _____
_____

📖

"To them God has chosen to make known among the Gentiles the glorious riches of this mystery, which is Christ in you, the hope of glory" (v. 27).

What is the task of the Saints, the Chosen? _____
_____

---

situation to achieve goals and results that are much higher and beyond our human perceptions and conceptions.

[165] Some may define this as the instructions given by God. What assignment(s) has God called you to? What directives has God given you in conjunction with other people belonging to God's family?

"We proclaim Him[166], admonishing and teaching everyone with all wisdom, so that we may present everyone perfect in Christ. To this end I labor, struggling with all His energy, which so powerfully works in me" (vv. 28-29).

How do the Saints complete their task (v. 28)?

1. _____
2. _____
3. _____
4. _____

As believers and saints of God are called to labor in the strength of God for who (v. 29)? _____
_____

---

[166] The world looks to the world for answers and thus remains lost in a desert of illusions, deceptions and lies. It gives credit to itself. It uplifts the things that are temporary and are subject to decay. It thrives in deceit. Thus, it is paramount that we proclaim reality; Jesus is the reason, Jesus is the source, Jesus is the truth, Jesus is life. Jesus alone should receive all the credit because Jesus is worthy of all the praise, adoration, and thanksgiving, because Jesus is God.

NOT ACCEPTED WISDOM BUT CHRIST: COLOSSIANS 2

CHAPTER BLUEPRINT

- The Two Churches   (2:1 – 2:5)
- Fullness in Christ   (2:6 – 2:15)
- Man's Adjudication is Worthless   (2:16 – 2:23)

THE TWO CHURCHES

"I want you to know how much I am struggling for you and for those at Laodicea[167], and for all who have not met me personally" (v.1).

Who is Paul struggling for? _____

_____

What are the two churches that Paul is addressing?

    1. _____

    2. _____

Where is Laodicea located? _____

_____

---

[167] This is a city that was known for its business market (export, import, buying and selling). The city was thought to be located about 11 miles north of Colosse. Both cities are known for sharing communication. The leaders of the church in Laodicea were called lukewarm (Revelation 3:16).

📖

"My purpose is that they may be encouraged in heart and united in love[168], so that they may have the full riches of complete understanding, in order that they may know the mystery of God[169], namely Christ, in whom are hidden all the treasures of wisdom and knowledge" (vv. 2-3).

What is the purpose of Paul (vv. 1-2)?

1. _____
2. _____
3. _____
4. _____
5. _____

What is hidden in Jesus (v. 3)? _____

_____

How does belief in Jesus Christ compare to Gnosticism (v. 3)? _____

_____

Because the weak are influenced by the strong, what should you avoid (2 Tim. 2:23)? _____

_____

📖

"I tell you this so that no one may deceive you by fine-sounding arguments[170]. For though I am absent from you in body, I am present with you in spirit

---

[168] There are so many people with various backgrounds, objectives, talents and gifts, and at various levels of spirituality that in the church. As a result, the church experiences much division and hurt. If Jesus is placed at the center of our lives and on the throne, the church can be united with each other yielding harmony, peace, focused and successful ministry. As a believer, where is your focus? Is Jesus at the center of all your endeavors? Are you causing division or reconciliation?

[169] The mystery of God refers to salvation also being available to the Gentiles, as well as, the Jews.

[170] The Gnostics conveyed that there was a knowledge that was hidden from the people, being that knowledge is the ultimate answer, and not Christ. People come to you with thoughts or arguments that seem to be true because they possess some augmented truths. But in examination, those arguments are false, created to deceive and destroy. Salvation in Jesus is available to all. Jesus extends

and delight to see how orderly you are and how firm your faith in Christ is" (vv. 4-5).

Why should one avoid disputes and arguments (v. 4)? _____
_____

How can we be with others in sprit (v. 5)? _____
_____

FULLNESS IN CHRIST

"So then, just as you received Christ Jesus as Lord, continue to live in Him, rooted and built up in Him, strengthened in the faith as you were taught, and overflowing with thankfulness" (vv. 6-7).

How did you receive Christ Jesus as Lord (v. 6)? _____
_____

What are we called to do (v. 6)? _____
_____

How are we to accomplish walking in the ways of Jesus (v. 7)?
1. _____
2. _____
3. _____
4. _____

"See to it that no one takes you captive through hollow and deceptive philosophy, which depends on human tradition and the basic principles of this world rather than on Christ[171]" (v. 8).

---

the gift of faith to all, and not just to the elite. Place your aspirations, your hope, and your destiny in faith of Jesus Christ, and not the knowledge or science of the world and deception of man.

[171] Human traditions can lead one away from Christ, away from worshiping in truth, away from studying God's word, and away from spending time with God in prayer and service. Why? Because the focused is on the tradition, the sacrament or man's viewpoint of obtaining deliverance, absolution or righteousness, which is not based on the word of God. If you keep your eyes on Jesus, and obeying His

How does the world take Christians captive or cheat Christians? _____

_____

The world depends on what?

1. _____
2. _____

📖

"For in Christ all the fullness of the Deity lives in bodily form, and you have been given fullness in Christ, who is the head over every power and authority[172]" (vv. 9-10).

Jesus is the fullness of whom (v. 9)? _____
What do we receive as a result of our faith in Jesus (v. 10)? _____

_____

What is the fullness in Christ that Paul is referring to?

1. Sin - _____
2. Life - _____
3. Forgiven - _____
4. Delivered - _____
5. Freed - _____

📖

"In Him you were also circumcised[173], in the putting off of the sinful nature, not with a circumcision done by the hands of men but with the circumcision done by Christ, having been buried with Him in baptism and raised with Him through your faith in the power of God, who raised Him from the dead" (vv. 11-12).

_____

    commandments, then captivity of man's ways and traditions will not overcome and control you.

[172] All of God's characteristics, attributes are in Christ because Jesus is God incarnate, which contradicts gnostic belief that there is a natural innate evil of physical bodies.

[173] Paul is talking about circumcision of the heart and spirit, and not of the tradition of the law which included the cutting away of the male foreskin.

How all Christians are circumcised (v. 11)? _____

_____

How does Jesus circumcise us (v. 12)?

    1. _____

    2. _____

When one receives Holy Communion, it symbolizes what? _____

_____

Who raised Jesus from the dead (v. 12)? _____

_____

📖

"When you were dead in your sins and in the uncircumcision of your sinful nature, God made you alive with Christ. He forgave us all our sins, having canceled the written code[174], with its regulations, that was against us and that stood opposed to us; He took it away, nailing it to the cross" (vv. 13-14).

When were you dead in sins (v. 13)? _____

_____

How did God make you alive in Christ (v. 13)? _____

What sins or trespasses did God forgive (v. 13)? _____

What was the handwriting or written code (v. 14)? _____

_____

What is the code of today that is canceled in regards to salvation? _____

_____

What did God do with the requirements (v. 14)? _____

_____

---

[174] Over the last several centuries, the forgiveness of sins has been a topic of argument between churches and theological scholars. God through Jesus and His word teaches and has demonstrated that true forgiveness of sins is only through Jesus Christ, and not through a ritual, a human or tradition.

"And having disarmed the powers and authorities[175], He made a public spectacle of them, triumphing over them by the cross" (v. 15).

What did God do to the powers and authorities? _____

_____

Who or what are the principalities and powers?

1. _____
2. _____
3. _____
4. _____
5. _____
6. _____
7. _____

MAN'S ADJUDICATION IS WORTHLESS

"Therefore do not let anyone judge you by what you eat or drink, or with regard to a religious festival, a New Moon celebration or a Sabbath day[176]. These are a shadow of the things that were to come; the reality, however, is found in Christ" (vv. 16-17).

As Christians, who should judge you regarding your rituals (v. 16)? _____

_____

Where is the substance or reality (v. 17)? _____

_____

---

[175] Suggestions have been made that this refers to all (Satan, leaders, fallen angels and governments) that was and is in opposition of Jesus.

[176] Mankind has a way of trying to determine who is righteous or holy by judging how well a person follows the traditions and celebrations. Do not get caught up in it. There is only one judge, and His name is Jesus.

"Do not let anyone who delights in false humility and the worship of angels disqualify you for the prize[177]. Such a person goes into great detail about what he has seen, and his unspiritual mind puffs him up with idle notions" (v. 18).

False humility and worship of angels was displayed by whom? _____
_____

False teachers can disqualify you for what? _____
False teachers possess a mindset that stems from what? _____
_____

Who are false teachers connected with?

1. _____
2. _____
3. _____
4. _____
5. _____

"He has lost connection with the Head[178], from whom the whole body, supported and held together by its ligaments and sinews, grows as God causes it to grow" (v. 19).

Who is the head and causes the whole body to grow? _____
_____

"Since you died with Christ to the basic principles of this world, why, as though you still belonged to it, do you submit to its rules: Do not handle! Do not taste! Do not touch!" (vv.20-21).

---

[177] If your humility is not in Christ Jesus, then it is false. Some people put on an act, in order to sway your heart and mind. Be alert to the false teachers, false leaders that will attempt to pull you from Jesus.

[178] If the head is cut off the body cannot function and there is no life. Are you connected with the head, which is Jesus Christ? Is Jesus the head of your life, hopes, expectations and objectives?

Paul C. Jones, PhD

What was the problem of the church at Colossae (v. 20)? _____
_____

Why Christians persists on submitting to living outside of Christ? _____
_____

What does God tell us to do in regards to the world and its rules and beliefs (v. 21)?

    1. _____
    2. _____
    3. _____

Man-made traditions and rules focus on what? _____
_____

Christianity focuses on what? _____

📖

"These are all destined to perish with use, because they are based on human commands and teachings. Such regulations indeed have an appearance of wisdom, with their self-imposed worship, their false humility and their harsh treatment of the body, but they lack any value in restraining sensual indulgence[179]" (vv. 22-23).

What is the result of worldly principles and beliefs (v. 22)? _____
_____

What is the indulgence of the flesh (v. 23)? _____
_____

---

[179] We cannot find God, true peace, purpose and meaning, understanding, wisdom or an abundant life through the ideologies, traditions, man-made spiritualties that insist on man's efforts, work, knowledge and practice. The work of Jesus and the cross is the only way in the eyes of God.

YOUR CHRISTIAN RESPONSE:
COLOSSIANS 3

CHAPTER BLUEPRINT
- Holy Policy   (3:1 – 3:11)
- Character of God's Chosen   (3:12 – 3:17)
- Rules for the Home   (3:18 – 3:25)

HOLY POLICY

"Since, then, you have been raised with Christ, set your hearts on things above[180], where Christ is seated at the right hand of God. Set your mind on things above, not on earthly things" (vv. 1-2).

To be raised with Christ assumes what (v. 1)? _____

_____

Does a person have to die with Christ in order to be raised with Christ? _

_____

What are the things that are above (v. 1)? _____

_____

"Where Christ is seated…" refers to what (v. 1)? _____

---

[180] On things above means that we must focused and think about the things that are unseen. The unseen things are the things that are holy and righteous. The earthly things or that which are seen are elements that will fade away, decay, or rot. The things that are seen are also temporary (i.e., money, assets, and emotions) and they result in despair, discord, darkness, depression, dismay, disappointment, defeat and death.

What are the earthly things (v. 2)? _____
_____

📖

"For you died[181], and your life is now hidden with Christ in God. When Christ, who is your life, appears, then you also will appear with Him in glory" (vv. 3-4).

How is your life hidden (v. 3)? _____

How is our Christian elements of this word that life the life of Christ (v. 4)? _____

When will you appear in glory (v. 4)? _____
_____

📖

"Put to death[182], therefore, whatever belongs to your earthly nature: sexual immorality, impurity, lust, evil desires and greed, which is idolatry. Because of these, the wrath of God is coming[183]" (vv. 5-6).

What are we supposed to put to death (v. 5)? _____
_____

Name 5 things that we are also to put t death (v. 5)?
    1. _____
    2. _____

---

[181] This is not referring to an actual death, but it pointing to the things that are of this world that use to be attractive, but are not important anymore. Those elements no longer have any appeal or benefit, they do not fulfill or bring joy, and have become a waste of resources. And now, your delight is in the Lord where you can find rest, joy, acceptance, value, and peace.

[182] Put to death means that we as believers should put forth every effort and bit of energy to refrain from.

[183] The opposite of God's blessings is His curse or wrath. This refers to the unhappy judgement that will come upon you from God for the practice of those behaviors.

3. _____

4. _____

5. _____

Covetousness or greed is also known as (v. 5)? _____

Why is the wrath of God coming (v. 6)? _____

_____

📖

"You used to walk in these ways, in the life you once lived" (v. 7).

Describe the life that we used to walk? _____

_____

📖

"But now you must rid yourselves of all such things as these: anger, rage, malice, slander, and filthy language from your lips[184]" (v. 8).

Name 5 things that we are to rid ourselves of?

1. _____

2. _____

3. _____

4. _____

5. _____

📖

"Do not lie to each other, since you have taken off your old self with its practices and have put on the new self, which is being renewed in knowledge in the image of its Creator[185]" (vv. 9-10).

---

[184] It's amazing how negative thoughts can lead one down a dark street that results in negative actions that brings injury to self and others, whether it is physical, psychological or in speech.

[185] When we lie, there is nothing positive that arises. Lies are temporal and are destructive. Even when you are stretching the truth just a little bit, the truth then becomes a lie and possesses the ability to bring harm, disappointment and separation. From God and those you love. It's not too late to make amends. Turn to the Lord and ask Him to transform you and mold you into what is pleasing and acceptable.

What shouldn't we do to each other (v. 9)? _____

What is the impact of lying? _____

_____

What is being renewed (v. 10)? _____

How is the "new self" being renewed (v. 10)? _____

_____

📖

"Here there is no Greek or Jew, circumcised or uncircumcised, barbarian, Scythian, slave or free, but Christ is all, and is in all[186]" (v. 11).

By naming Greek, Jew, Circumcised...God is stating what? _____

_____

What does it mean that Christ is all? _____

_____

What does it mean that Christ is in all? _____

_____

CHARACTER OF GOD'S CHOSEN

"Therefore, as God's chosen people, holy and dearly loved, clothe yourselves with compassion, kindness, humility, gentleness and patience[187]" (v.12).

What is the status of God's people? _____
What should Christians do?

1. _____
2. _____
3. _____
4. _____
5. _____

---

[186] There are no favorites. In God's family, all are welcomed regardless of your status, background, ethnicity, gender or age. All believers belong to Jesus, and Jesus lives within each believer.

[187] These attributes are synonymous with the Fruit of the Spirit (Galatians 5:22) that should consume our very being and interactions, and be our product.

"Bear with each other and forgive whatever grievances you may have against one another[188]. Forgive as the Lord forgave you[189]. And over all these virtues put on love, which binds them all together in perfect unity" (vv. 13-14).

How do you bear with those who wrong you (v. 13)? _____
_____

How are we supposed to forgive (v. 13)? _____
_____

What is the function of love (v. 14)? _____
_____

"Let the peace of Christ rule in your hearts, since as members of one body you were called to peace[190]. And be thankful" (v.15).

What should rule in our hearts? _____
What is meant by "rule"? _____
_____

What is the Peace of God/Christ? _____
_____

All Christians or believers are called to what? _____
All Christians or believers are called to do what? _____

---

[188] To bear means to tolerate and endure. It is a byproduct of having patience and finding contentment in the situation.

[189] When we remember how the Lord forgave us, what He forgave us for, and how many times the Lord has forgiven us, forgiveness of others becomes a way of life and not a struggle.

[190] God created each person differently, with different gifts and talents. However, as believers, we have become one family in God, connected to one body in Christ Jesus. Just as your body has many parts but belong to the same body, all Christians, regardless of location or status, belong to God's body and family.

📖

"Let the word of Christ dwell in you richly as you teach and admonish one another with all wisdom[191], and as you sing psalms, hymns and spiritual songs with gratitude in your hearts to God" (v.16).

Where should the word of God dwell? _____

To dwell richly means what? _____

_____

With Wisdom, what are we supposed to do?

1. _____
2. _____
3. _____
4. _____
5. _____
6. _____
7. _____

📖

"And whatever you do, whether in word or deed, do it all in the name of the Lord Jesus, giving thanks to God the Father through Him" (v.17).

Whatever we do, we do it how? _____

In the name of Jesus means what? _____

_____

How do we give thanks to God the Father? _____

_____

RULES FOR THE HOME

"Wives, submit to your husbands, as is fitting in the Lord. Husbands, love your wives and do not be harsh with them[192]. Children, obey your parents

---

[191] To admonish means to criticize. We can criticize to destroy or we can provide positive constructive criticism, which comes from wisdom, which builds up and encourages.

[192] This advice for relationship is not a command for dictatorship or to give power and control of one over the other. It is a reminder and manner that as family

in everything, for this pleases the Lord. Fathers, do not embitter your children, or they will become discouraged[193]" (vv. 18-21).

How should wives submit to their husbands (v. 18)? _____

_____

How should husbands treat their wives (v. 19)? _____

_____

How can children please the Lord (v. 20)? _____

_____

Why shouldn't fathers provoke their children (v. 21)? _____

_____

📖

"Slaves, obey your earthly masters in everything; and do it, not only when their eye is on you and to win their favor, but with sincerity of heart and reverence for the Lord" (v. 22).

In what manner is slavery being supported, if any? _____

_____

How are slaves or servants supposed to act? _____

_____

📖

"Whatever you do, work at it with all our heart, as working for the Lord[194], not for men, since you know that you will receive an inheritance from the Lord as a reward. It is the Lord Christ you are serving" (vv. 23-24).

---

members, we need to give of what we have to each other for the good, working with each other out of respect and love for each other and for God.

[193] Words have a way of inciting action. It is paramount that words of the parent be chosen carefully in order to avoid negative response from the children or a responses that give bring harm and hurt. This is also good advice for couples in how they interact with each other; no provoking, no fighting.

[194] Working for the Lord should not be something that is taxing and causes irritability. Working for the Lord should be bring an internal joy, inspiration and zeal to live more for Jesus, knowing that you are participating in the will of God being fulfilled.

To work with all your heart is a command for whom (v. 23)? _____
_____

And what attitude should all Christians hold when they work (v. 23)? ___
_____

Our inheritance is what (v. 24)? _____
In essence, who are we serving when we serve mankind (v. 24)? _____
_____

📖

"Anyone who does wrong will be repaid for his wrong, and there is no favoritism" (v. 25).

What happens to those who do wrong? _____
_____

Will God show partiality or favoritism toward Christians verses non-Christians when they do wrong (v. 25)? _____

SPECIAL DUTIES: COLOSSIANS 4

CHAPTER BLUEPRINT

FAIR TREATMENT

Masters, provide your slaves with what is right and fair, because you know that you also have a Master in heaven" (v. 1).

How should masters treat servants or slaves? _____

_____

What is the standard of rule to follow regarding the treatment of others?

_____

CHRISTIAN DECENCY

"Devote yourselves to prayer[195], being watchful and thankful. And pray for us, too, that God may open a door for our message, so that we may proclaim the mystery of Christ[196], for which I am in chains" (vv. 2-3).

We are to continue earnestly or devote ourselves to(v. 2)? _____

How can one be vigilant or watchful in prayer (v. 2)? _____

According to Paul, who should we include in prayer (v. 3)? _____

Who are "us" (v. 3)?
1. _____
2. _____
3. _____
4. _____

Why is Paul requesting prayer (v. 3)? _____

Who creates the opportunity for the Word to be heard or received (v. 3)?

What is the "mystery of Christ" (v. 3)? _____

What does Paul mean when he states that he is in chains (v. 3)? _____

---

[195] Prayer is a means of communication between you, God the Father, God the Son and God the Holy Spirit. Through prayer, one finds healing, answers, petitions, strength, hope, comfort, assurance, intimacy, deliverance, joy, self-control, understanding, wisdom and peace, whether the prayer is for self or for others. What do you find through your prayer life? How much time do you give to prayer?

[196] The mystery of Christ is the message of the gospel or good news. That is, it is the working of God's deliverance and redemption of mankind to all who will listen and believe.

📖

"Pray that I may proclaim it clearly, as I should. Be wise in the way you act toward outsiders; make the most of every opportunity[197]" (vv. 4-5).

What problem could there be in proclaiming the Word (v. 4)? _____

_____

To "be wise" or "walk in wisdom" toward outsiders means what (v. 5)? __

_____

📖

"Let your conversation be always full of grace, seasoned with salt[198], so that you may know how to answer everyone" (v. 6).

How one you be gracious in delivering the Word of God? _____

_____

To be "seasoned with salt" means what? _____

_____

Describe the environment whereby you feel comfortable talking about God? _____

_____

GREETINGS

"Tychicus will tell you all the news about me. He is a dear brother, a faithful minister and fellow servant in the Lord. I am sending him to you

---

[197] To be wise in this case means to be alert and sensible to how you respond to people who are not in the family of believers and surroundings. Everyday there are opportunities for you to witness to others through your words, actions and even thoughts. The manner in which we act can cause someone to turn away from the message and miss the opportunity to have a relationship with God through Jesus Christ. The scripture tells us (Matthew 5:16) to, "let our light shine before men, that they may see your good deeds and praise your Father in heaven."

[198] Salt is more than an element that boost flavor. Salt is an element that preserves. Our words should consist of spiritually dense language that preserves, protects, encourages and helps endure.

for the express purpose that you may know about our circumstances and that he may encourage your hearts[199]" (vv. 7-8).

Who is Tychicus [Tike-e-cus] (vv. 7-8)?

1. _____
2. _____
3. _____
4. _____
5. _____

"He is coming with Onesimus, our faithful and dear brother, who is one of you. They will tell you everything that is happening here" (v. 9).

Who is Onesimus [O-nes-i-mus]?

1. _____
2. _____
3. _____
4. _____
5. _____

"My fellow prisoner Aristarchus sends you his greetings, as does Mark, the cousin of Barnabas. You have received instructions about him; if he comes to you, welcome him" (v. 10).

Who is Aristarchus [Aris-tar-kus]?

1. _____ (Acts 19:29)
2. _____ (Acts 20:4)
3. _____ (Acts 20:4)
4. _____ (Acts 27:2)
5. _____

---

[199] The lesson of proclaiming the gospel is emphasized. The ministry of the Lord is not an act that is performed by one person only. It requires the work of many members, at various times, in different places, and with varying gifts and talents. Are you open and ready to share the good news of the Lord in your daily living? Or are you depending on someone else?

Mark is known for what three things?

1. _____
2. _____
3. _____

Paul names eight people to remind us of what (vv. 7-15)? _____

_____

📖

"Jesus[200], who is called Justus, also sends greetings. These are the only Jews among my fellow workers for the kingdom of God, and they have proved a comfort to me" (v. 11).

Is the Jesus mentioned in this verse the same as Jesus Christ? _____

_____

📖

"Epaphras, who is one of you and a servant of Christ Jesus, sends greetings. He is always wrestling in prayer for you, that you may stand firm in all the will of God, mature and full assured. I vouch for him that he is working hard for you and for those at Laodicea and Hierapolis" (vv. 12-13).

If we are like Epaphras, what should we do (v. 12)? _____

_____

Where s Laodicea located (v. 13)? _____

_____

Where is Hierapolis located (v. 13)? _____

_____

Colossae is located where? _____

📖

"Our dear friend Luke, the doctor, and Demas send greetings. Give my greetings to the brothers at Laodicea, and to Nympha and the church in her house" (vv. 14-15).

---

[200] Jesus was the surname of a friend of Paul and a co-worker of the gospel whose name was Justus.

Who is Luke (v. 14)?

1. _____
2. _____
3. _____

Demas is known for what (v. 14)? _____

_____

(Hint: 2 Timothy 4:10)_____

_____

The story of Demas reminds Christians of what? _____

_____

This revelation of Nympha opens the boundaries of what (v. 15)? _____

_____

BLESSINGS

"After this letter has been read to you, see that it is also read in the church of the Laodiceans and that you in turn read the letter from Laodicea[201]" (v. 16).

The Word of God is meant for who? _____

_____

"See to it that you complete the work you have received in the Lord" (v. 17).

Why do we leave our work/ministry undone or unfulfilled?

1. _____
2. _____
3. _____
4. _____
5. _____
6. _____

---

[201] We don't have the letter from Laodicea. It is thought that there were several letters written between the churches that have not been found. But we can suggest, by what we have, that the letters were ones to encourage, clarify, bless and lift up the supremacy of Jesus Christ, who is God.

7. _____

"I, Paul, write this greeting in my own hand. Remember my chains. Grace be with you" (v. 18).

Why does Paul mention about writing this greeting/salutation in his own hand?

1. _____
2. _____

How does Paul end the letter? _____

_____

Philemon

OVERVIEW AND OUTLINE OF PHILEMON

Who is the Author: _____

When was the book written (B.C., A.D): _____

From what location was the book written? _____

What number is the book in the New Testament & Canonical Bible:

Setting or Location: _____

What was the main purpose of this letter? _____

BOOK BLUEPRINT

- **Appreciation of Philemon**   Verses 1-7
- **Plea to Onesimus**   Verses 8-25

MAJOR ARGUMENTS[202]

As Christians, we are called to restore one another, which demands the act and heart of forgiveness, regardless of relationship or gender. This heart must be filled with compassion for others, as well as, for self in order for healing and understanding to manifest itself. Yet, time and time again society is faced with unbalanced scales that obstructs are focus on God.

Slavery, or the position of being a servant, can be a barrier that presents a division among one another, as well as, being an element that can separate people from God. As Christians, there should not be any walls (political,

---

[202] Life Application Study Bible, New International Version, Tyndale House Publishers, Inc. and Zondervan Publishing House, 1988, 1989, 1990, 1991

racial, economic, geographical, age, education or gender) to separate us from one another. In Christ we are all one family. When you extend mercy and empathy, when you make pleas in Christian love, the manner that you act should be with sensitive and thoughtful arguments, which exhibits to the recipient worth in the eyes of others, self and God.

2 FORGIVENESS: PHILEMON 1

CHAPTER BLUEPRINT

- Greeting   (1:1 – 1:3)
- Prayer   (1:4 – 1:7)
- Entreaty for Onesimus   (1:8 – 1:16)
- Encouragement   (1:17 – 1:22)
- Blessings   (1:23 – 1:25)

GREETING

"Paul, a prisoner of Christ Jesus[203], and Timothy our brother[204], to Philemon our dear friend and fellow worker[205], to Apphia our sister, to Archippus our fellow soldier and to the church that meets in your home" (vv. 1-2).

---

[203] Paul was not an actual prisoner bound in chains and restraints by Jesus, but Paul had been imprisoned in Rome for trusting and obeying Jesus. Paul was determined to serve Jesus, fight the cause and spread the gospel throughout the land. Throughout your day and your routine, are you exerting the effort to tell people about the good news? The love of Jesus?

[204] Timothy was a close associate of Paul that studied and was guided by Paul. Timothy was thought of as his brother, son and friend, willing to be used and sent by God. Have you determine in your heart and mind to put serving the Lord first and confess, here am I Lord, send me?

[205] Philemon, by all account, was a member of the church in Colossae and owned land. He was the master over Onesimus. It has been stated in various ways throughout circles and history that you become a slave to whatever controls your speech, thoughts, actions, decisions and time.

Paul is what (v.1)? _____

_____

Opening greeting is to whom (vv. 1-2)?
1. _____
2. _____
3. _____
4. _____
5. _____

Who is Apphia (v. 2)? _____

Who is Archippus (v. 2)? _____

_____

📖

"Grace to you and peace from God our Father and the Lord Jesus Christ" (v. 3)

What is the greeting and blessing? _____

_____

PRAYER

"I always thank my God as I remember you in my prayers, because I hear about your faith in the Lord Jesus and your love for all the saints[206]" (vv. 4-5).

What does Paul do that we should also do (v. 4)? _____

_____

Why does Paul thank God for the people (v. 5)?
1. _____
2. _____

---

[206] There are so many types of prayers, but a prayer that uplifts with thanksgiving and appreciation stirs the soul and encourages. Whenever we hear good news of those who are doing God's will and are growing in faith and love, we should lift them up to the Lord for strength, focus and commitment.

How often do you thank God for the people for the same reason Paul does? _____

_____

📖

"I pray that you may be active in sharing your faith, so that you will have a full understanding of every good thing we have in Christ[207]. Your love has given me great joy and encouragement, because you, brother, have refreshed the hearts of the saints[208]" (vv. 6-7).

What is one of the things Paul prays for (v. 6)? _____

_____

Name some ways you can be "active" or "effective" in sharing your faith:
1. _____
2. _____
3. _____
4. _____
5. _____

Why does Paul share his faith (v. 7)? _____

_____

What happens when you share with someone else (v. 7)? _____

_____

ENTREATY FOR ONESIMUS

"Therefore, although in Christ I could be bold and order you to do what you ought to do, yet I appeal to you on the basis of love; I then, as Paul, an old man and now also a prisoner of Christ Jesus" (vv. 8-9)
Entreaty means what? _____

---

[207] When you share your faith, you share by the power of the Holy Spirit, who guides you to all truth and all that is beneficial in Christ. When you share Jesus, do you ask the Holy Spirit to guide your tongue?

[208] What does your love do for others? Does it empower, encourage or invigorate? Does it celebrate and bring joy?

Paul C. Jones, PhD

What is Paul stating about exercising authority (vv. 8-9)? _____
_____

Christians should always give advice in what manner (v. 9)? _____
Onesimus means what? _____

📖

"I appeal to you for my son Onesimus, who became my son while I was in chains[209]. Formerly he was useless to you, but now he has become useful both to you and me" (vv. 10-11).

How did Onesimus become a "son" of Paul (v. 10)? _____
_____

Why was Onesimus useless in the past (v. 11)? _____
_____

How is Onesimus useful to Paul and Philemon (v. 11)? _____
_____

📖

"I am sending him who is my very heart back to you. I would have liked to keep him with me so that he could take your place in helping me while I am in chains for the gospel[210]" (vv. 12-13).

Who is Paul sending back to Philemon (v. 12)? _____
Why was Paul hesitant in sending Onesimus (v. 13)? _____
_____

[209] While Paul was incarcerated, it appears that Onesimus accepted Jesus as his Savior in light of Paul's witness. Although Paul and Onesimus became brothers in the Lord, a relationship was established as in teacher to student or father to son.

[210] Paul was utilizing Philemon to help in the ministry. Paul saw another opportunity in Onesimus. It is nice and we feel good when we accept the Lord. But if we keep the blessings of the Lord to ourselves, what good is it to society, the unchurch or unsaved? We, as Christians, are to be instruments for God's word to go out into the world, which may mean traveling to places that may not be desirable.

"But I did not want to do anything without your consent, so that any favor you do will be spontaneous and not forced[211]. Perhaps the reason he was separated from you for a little while was that you might have him back for good, no longer a slave, but better that a slave, as a dear brother. He is very dear to me but even dearer to you, both as a man and as a brother in the Lord[212]" (vv. 14-16).

We should always receive consent from whom (v. 14)? _____

_____

Service that we extend to others should be what (v. 14)? _____

Philemon was instructed to receive Onesimus how (vv. 15-16)? _____

_____

Christians are to receive one another in what manner? _____

_____

ENCOURAGEMENT

"So if you consider me a partner, welcome him as you would welcome me[213]. If he has done you any wrong or owes you anything, charge it to me" (vv. 17-18).

People are called to welcome each other in what mode (v. 17)? _____

_____

What is the overall message of Paul in this verse (v. 18)? _____

_____

---

[211] It is so important to have consent or permission. Consent keeps unity and peace. Consent fosters trust and enhanced relationships. Jesus, himself, did not do anything without going to the Father first. Are you acting out of your own will and desire, or are you obtaining consent from your heavenly Father?

[212] Our value is not determined or gauged by our assessments, successes, or what the world defines as worth. Our value is established by God, who is the Creator and the One who gives the increase. Do you describe yourself by your accomplishments, gifts or talents, or by who you are in Christ Jesus?

[213] Hospitality should always be at the forefront. It doesn't cost anything to be kind, loving, gentle, appreciative and welcoming. God's love is perceived and made visible as we extend ourselves to others.

"I, Paul am writing this with my own hand. I will pay it back, not to mention that you owe me your very self" (v. 19).

Why does Paul state about writing with his own hand? _____
_____

What did it mean that Philemon owed Paul? _____
_____

"I do wish, brother, that I may have some benefit from you in the Lord; refresh my heart in Christ" (v. 20).

What benefit is Paul referring to? _____
_____

When someone does well for us, we should respond how? _____
_____

"Confident of your obedience[214], I write to you, knowing that you will do even more than I ask. And one thing more: prepare a guest room for me, because I hope to be restored to you in answer to your prayers" (vv. 21-22).

Christ calls His servants to do what (v. 21)? _____
As Christians, we should always be prepared for what (v. 22)? _____
_____

BLESSINGS

"Epaphras[215], my fellow prisoner in Christ Jesus, sends you greetings. And so do Mark, Aristarchus, Demas and Luke, my fellow workers" (vv. 23-24).

---

[214] Confidence is established through past experiences, knowledge of capabilities along with expectations. Paul was assure that the heart in Philemon and his love of Jesus would inspire him to a point beyond basic satisfaction, but to aspire to higher heights of deeds.

[215] Epaphras was a known servant (minister) of the Lord in the area who started the church in Colossae. It is thought that he might have been converted through Paul.

What does Epaphras, Mark, Aristarchus, Demas and Luke have in common (vv. 23-24)?

1. _____
2. _____
3. _____
4. _____
5. _____

"The grace of the Lord Jesus Christ be with your spirit" (v. 25).

What is Paul's final blessing? _____

_____

Printed in the United States
By Bookmasters